T0355883

PRAISE FOR
THE SOCCER OF SUCCESS

I never thought I would ever recommend taking advice from an Englishman, let alone a Manchester United fan. However, I have personally witnessed the incredible business that Ciarán has built and sold. He is respected for his genuine commitment to soccer, his community, and family. It is a rare opportunity to have a great leader allow you to peek into their playbook, do not miss this chance!

— **Brendan Moylan**
Co-founder, SOCCER.COM

You don't have to be a professional player to love and understand the game. Ciarán has embraced this and written a book for all soccer fans who want to use the lessons from the game as tools for success, in business and life.

— **Robbie Mustoe**
Premier League Studio Analyst, NBC Sports

Ciarán's enlightening insights brilliantly show how the beautiful game's wisdom can lead to extraordinary achievement. It's a must-read for any soccer fan who is passionately pursuing excellence in all facets of their life.

— **Michelyne Pinard**
Coach of three-time NCAA Champions

As a former professional who encountered a few challenges when transitioning from the routine of professional sport, I feel like this book offers a succinct understanding to help others realize the transferable skills they have developed in their previous field, which can assist them in making the transition into the next chapter of their life a more manageable journey. Alternatively, if you are just starting out on your new venture or life change, the steps are there in the book to help you navigate this unpredictable terrain.

— **Gary Teale**
Former English Premier League and Scottish National Team Player

Ciarán's background and clear passion for soccer have inspired a unique exploration of life's challenges and triumphs through the lens of the beautiful game. With keen insight and clear analogies, he investigates how the soccer pitch mirrors our own journeys, offering invaluable lessons to help on our everyday pursuit of victory. A very interesting read that will make you reflect and act!

— **Luiz Muzzi**
GM and Executive VP, Soccer Ops, Orlando City Soccer Club, Major League Soccer

Following a twenty-year professional career, Ciarán's book has allowed me to take all the lessons from the game and translate them perfectly into business fundamentals, which has helped me tremendously in my post-playing career.

— Alan Smith

Premier League Winner and England International

Ciarán has written a fantastic book for every soccer fan that teaches them how to plan, perform, and recover in both the long and short term, to ensure success in both business and life.

— Ally Mackay

General manager, DC United, Major League Soccer

THE SOCCER OF SUCCESS

CIARÁN McARDLE

THE
SOCCER
OF
SUCCESS

HOW THE BEAUTIFUL GAME CAN
HELP YOU ACHIEVE GOALS
IN BUSINESS & LIFE

Forbes | Books

Published by Forbes Books, Charleston, South Carolina.
An imprint of Advantage Media Group.

Forbes Books is a registered trademark, and the Forbes Books colophon is a trademark of Forbes Media, LLC.

Printed in the United States of America.

10 9 8 7 6 5 4 3 2 1

ISBN: 979-8-88750-523-7 (Hardcover)
ISBN: 979-8-88750-524-4 (eBook)

Library of Congress Control Number: 2024916565

Cover design by Lance Buckley.
Layout design by Ruthie Wood.

This custom publication is intended to provide accurate information and the opinions of the author in regard to the subject matter covered. It is sold with the understanding that the publisher, Forbes Books, is not engaged in rendering legal, financial, or professional services of any kind. If legal advice or other expert assistance is required, the reader is advised to seek the services of a competent professional.

Since 1917, Forbes has remained steadfast in its mission to serve as the defining voice of entrepreneurial capitalism. Forbes Books, launched in 2016 through a partnership with Advantage Media, furthers that aim by helping business and thought leaders bring their stories, passion, and knowledge to the forefront in custom books. Opinions expressed by Forbes Books authors are their own. To be considered for publication, please visit **books.Forbes.com**.

CONTENTS

INTRODUCTION

Somebody said that football's a matter of life and death ... I said, "Listen, it's more important than that."

—BILL SHANKLY

I remember right where I was on May 26, 1999. I was in the Crimson Sports Grille in Harvard Square, surrounded by a few of my fellow Brits. I was working my first full-time job as a coach for local soccer players, and my friends were playing on the Harvard team. We'd gathered around to watch the Champions League final: my team, Manchester United, versus Bayern Munich.

It was a tough watch for much of the game. United's captain, Roy Keane, was suspended, as was their midfield maestro, Paul Scholes. Munich took advantage early through Mario Basler's free kick. The rest of the first half was cagey. United continued to struggle for an answer to that opening goal through most of the second half. Goalkeeper Peter Schmeichel had to work to keep the team in the match.

Then, United's manager, Sir Alex Ferguson, made a couple of brilliant substitutions. First, he brought on Teddy Sheringham in the sixty-seventh minute. Sheringham had spent much of the season coming off the bench. Suddenly, he was being trusted with reviving

United's flagging chances to win the match and complete the treble. Sheringham had just scored in the FA Cup final four days earlier. The hope was he could do it again.

But the chance didn't come right away. The minutes ticked away. Then, with only ten minutes left in the game, Ferguson introduced Ole Gunnar Solskjaer.

The rest is a matter of legend. You can probably fill in the details yourself. A minute into injury time, Sheringham latched onto the ball after a weak shot from Ryan Giggs. He shepherded it into the net and brought United 1-1.

Two minutes later, United had a corner. Beckham sent the ball into the box, Sheringham headed it on, and Ole Gunnar Solskjaer stuck his foot out at just the right moment to send the ball into the top of the net and win the match.

Football, bloody hell.

Soccer Is So Much More than a Sport

It's a great story—one of those moments that every soccer fan loves, whether you support Man U or not. And it was only possible because United got their timing right. Ferguson made the right substitutions at the right moments in the game. Sheringham and Solskjaer timed their movements perfectly to be just in the right place at the right moment to score the two goals that made the difference.

So much of soccer is like that. If a forward starts their run a millisecond early, they're offside—a millisecond late, and the defender gets to the ball first. Jump too early or too late and a striker misses a key header. A mistimed tackle can lead to a red card or an open goal.

It's the same in life. Open a business at the wrong moment, and even a great product can fail. Show up five minutes late to a meeting, and you can watch a sale transform into a missed opportunity. On the other hand, if you get your timing perfect, it can completely transform your potential. Myspace came along a little too early. Facebook arrived right on time. The latter is now one of the biggest companies in the world.

This is why the beautiful game lends itself so well to lessons in business and life. The qualities you need for success on the pitch are the same ones you need for success in every other aspect of life. The habits that allow a soccer player to excel are the same that allow an entrepreneur to reach the top or a parent to raise a great kid. The same commitment to constant improvement that allows a young talent to become an all-star also allows a salesperson to outsell their entire department and a middle-aged person to get in shape and run a marathon.

In this book, we'll cover all the insights we can gain from the beautiful game—insights that can make you a success across your whole life, whether you're an athlete dreaming of a debut under the Old Trafford flood lights, an entrepreneur with a dream of disrupting an industry, or a stay-at-home parent looking to maximize the quality of life for everyone in the family. We'll look at how you can organize yourself so you're always doing the most important work first and how you can make sure you always have the energy and focus to perform as soon as the whistle blows in your life. We'll look at the mentality required to perform and the frameworks you can use to improve on that performance a little bit each day. We'll consider the need for rest and reviewing your progress, as well as how you overcome failure, how you build on your strengths, and how you assemble a team you can lead to a championship.

And that's just the beginning.

Breaking the Game Down

Like a ball passed into the box, advice is often only as good as its delivery. Even good advice can come across as dry, irrelevant, or unactionable. No manager in soccer or business is going to get the performance they're looking for out of their team simply by shouting, "Everyone, try a little bit harder." A great manager knows that communication is an art. You have to deliver the key insights at the right time in a way that sticks with people.

This is why soccer is such a great vehicle for delivering lessons about successful living. Beyond the joy the game brings us, it offers us a chance to go deeper, understanding ideas that can change our lives concretely and giving us the blueprint to act on those ideas more effectively—all while making the process a lot more fun.

Consider that simple advice: "Everyone, try a little bit harder." It's absolutely true that if everyone pulls in the same direction and works a little harder, it can make all the difference. But simply telling a team that doesn't do much good.

Instead, imagine breaking that idea down to your team using the example of closing out a game in injury time. That's when a game is really won or lost—as United proved in 1999. In those final minutes, the little things make all the difference. Finding the legs to burst past a defender can open up that one big chance. Closing down an opponent racing for your goal can secure a result.

Every fan knows this instinctively, and that can allow them to draw the lesson from it and connect it to their own lives. For your company, "closing out the game" might be a matter of holding the door open for every client or making that one last call before leaving for the evening. Whatever it is, everyone knows it immediately simply by putting themselves in that scenario.

Preseason for the Mind

The lessons we gain from this sport can change our professional fortunes. They can also affect how we relate to our family and how we take care of ourselves. Soccer players are among the most elite performers on the planet. If we take the right lessons from them, we, too, can perform at the highest level—whatever we're trying to achieve.

That's what we're aiming to do here. Each chapter in the book is designed to provide a lesson we see exhibited on the pitch every week. You can think of this as your preseason training guide for your mind. Follow this training regimen, and you are in the best possible position to succeed on day one of your season—giving you your best shot at winning the championship. Your season may be starting college or a new job. It may involve moving into entrepreneurship or leadership. It could be starting a family or starting a new school year. No matter what your goals, a great preseason can whip you into shape for the work ahead.

And keep in mind, preseason is not one and done in this sport. You need one before every season. Whatever season your life is moving into, these tools can make the difference.

In fact, over time, these tools build on each other and allow you to keep improving, no matter how your goals shift. Sir Dave Brailsford, one of the leaders currently restructuring Manchester United, became famous for his marginal gains philosophy. According to this idea, small improvements in multiple areas can net massive improvements over time. Using this idea, Brailsford helped British cycling win their first gold medals in almost a hundred years. He used the same idea to win the Tour de France multiple times for Team Sky.

This book has a similar philosophy. Getting even marginally better at time management, organization, and avoiding distractions;

improving your health, your comprehension, and your leadership skills—all of this will make you more successful in life. This is the key to peak performance.

Of course, peak performance is going to look different for everyone reading this book. Some of you are looking for a big promotion; others are hoping to start your own company. Some want to take better care of your finances; others would love to run a 5K at a respectable time. Whatever you are looking to achieve, though, the lessons here are designed to help you achieve it.

And they are also designed to show immediate improvement. Every lesson is fully actionable, including exercises to get you moving in the right direction right away. The chapters are organized to add improvement upon improvement, but it's equally possible to jump in at any point and start with the lessons you need most.

Every team trains a little differently ahead of a big season. You can set your own training regimen here.

Meet the Coach

A keen reader will notice that I've been referring to the sport mostly as soccer so far. This is because, despite being born and raised in England, I've built my career in America, where calling the sport "football" can be a bit confusing. It's worth pointing out, though, even as just an aside, that "soccer" is a British term coined in the 1880s to distinguish it from "rugger"—rugby as we'd call it now—another form of "football" to add to the mix. Soccer is now the preferred term in most countries that have another popular form of football, such as Ireland, South Africa, and Australia.

But that's neither here nor there really. The point is that soccer has always been more than a hobby or an interest to me. I've made my career around it. I've founded and grown multiple businesses at the center of the soccer world. I'm the CEO and cofounder of XL Soccer World, a leading sports facility management and sports travel company. I've grown XL Soccer World into ten premier facilities welcoming more than three million visitors annually. I recently executed the opening of a new $10 million Orlando flagship facility. I've also opened XL Academy, a fully accredited school and soccer academy for young players who dream of going pro.

And as much as it pains me to say it, our company has done so well that we were recently acquired by Sofive, which is majority owned by City Football Group.

My career has been one of constant reinvention, moving from travel to facility management to education—and now, to author. I've been able to reinvent myself successfully so many times because of the lessons in this book.

That's the kind of potential these lessons can unleash in your life. I can't guarantee you'll succeed in your endeavors, but the ideas ahead can give you a clear shot on goal to achieve them. Of course, some shots skyrocket over the bar, and some shots are saved. But having a clear opening to take your shot gives you the chance to show what you're made of. And with these lessons, you've got the best opportunity to really score a worldie.

PART I

Plan

CHAPTER 1

The Hat Trick of Success

Much of what a manager does at a soccer club involves planning. They plan for which players the team needs to purchase and sell in the next transfer window. They plan for the season with training and tactical focus. They plan for each match. In fact, they plan in more detail than I could possibly fit in this chapter.

They plan everything in order to allow the players to perform.

But that's not quite the whole story. The manager has another key role to play: they review and adjust. Think of all the great substitutions managers have made in the big, classic games we all remember. It's not just Sir Alex subbing in Sheringham and Solskjaer in 1999. Look at Zinedine Zidane bringing on Gareth Bale in the Champions League final against Liverpool in 2018. Not only did Bale's bicycle kick win the game and the trophy, but it was also one of the best goals the competition has ever seen. Or consider Bobby Robson bringing on John Barnes for England in the 1986 World Cup semifinal against Argentina. With little more than ten minutes left, Barnes earned an assist and nearly had another. That would have allowed England to come back against Maradona (playing maybe the best game of soccer in history) and "the hand of God."

Managers also review midseason. While it's generally not preferable, great managers have been known to make key purchases in the January transfer market that can transform the whole season. Jürgen Klopp bought Virgil van Dijk in January, a defender so good he helped bring Liverpool their first title in decades. Bruno Fernandes came to Manchester United in 2020 and became United's best signing since Sir Alex retired.

This is why managers are so important within a club. They don't just make a plan and stick to it. They plan, they build the team to perform, and then they review progress and make the changes that can lead to titles and glory.

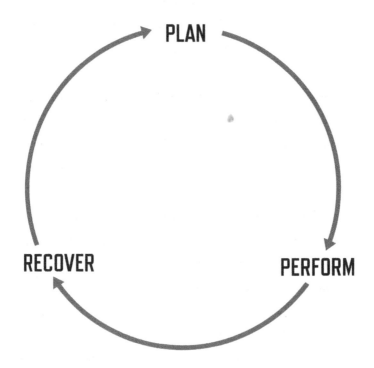

Plan, Perform, Recover

Everywhere you look in soccer, you'll notice the same pattern. It's plan, perform, and recover. Before a season, the manager plans. The team performs over the season. Afterward, the manager reviews and replaces players in the squad while the players recover. Before a game, there's a plan; during the game, there's a performance; and after the game, the players recover and review how they did. When a club seeks out a new manager, they plan for who would best fit, they allow the manager to perform, and then they review whether the manager has done well enough.

It's the same cycle over and over again. The reason is obvious: it allows individuals and teams to perform at their highest level. Plan, perform, recover is a hat trick of activities most likely to lead to success.

And this isn't just useful within the game. If you want to be successful in anything, you have to perform this hat trick yourself. If you have a big meeting next week, you should plan for it, perform during the meeting, and review that performance afterward. If you're welcoming a new child into your family, you should plan for parenthood, perform in the role, and review how you're doing every now and again. It also doesn't hurt to take some time to recover when you have a free moment—get some extra sleep, sneak in a date night with your spouse, spend a little time with friends.

This cycle offers the opportunity for success in every season of your life. It's there for your short-term and long-term goals, as well as your important and lower-priority aims. It works so effectively because it feeds into itself. Each element is equally important. Each piece builds on the others. Planning allows you to perform at a higher level. Performance gives meaning to planning. Recovery and review allow you to regain energy and learn lessons from your performance that can then influence your next round of planning.

Equally, removing any step makes your success more fragile. Going into any situations without planning increases the likelihood you underperform. Skipping recovery increases the likelihood you burn out or get injured. Failing to review increases the likelihood you repeat the same mistakes. And all the planning in the world comes to nothing if we never perform.

Every stage of the hat trick of success has to be in place if we want to reach our goals. And that's true across every goal you set. Soccer managers use this same cycle within a game, between games, in a tournament, across a season, and over a dynasty. You can use it to get in shape, to start a business, to learn a musical instrument, or to go on a vacation.

No matter where you're heading, the hat trick of success helps get you there.

That's why we start here. This is no Soccer of Success without the hat trick of success.

Strengthen Every Part of the Cycle

I've shaped this book around the hat trick of success. We'll start with tools to improve your planning before jumping into those that can help you perform and then those that will allow you to review and recover. We'll end by considering how you can take these lessons beyond yourself and integrate them into a team.

But I want to make it clear here that you don't have to follow these chapters in order. Each one can offer new ways to improve your process of achieving everything you want to across your whole life.

So follow what interests you most or where you feel you're most deficient. Take a little here and there or go through chapter by chapter. No matter how you use the tools ahead, they will improve the cycle that gets you where you want to go.

Game Time

At the end of each chapter, I'll provide some "game time" actionable steps you can use to begin working in each area.

Here, I want you to think of the one thing that is stressing you out the most at this moment. Now, think of the single next actionable step that you would need to complete in order to eventually solve the problem.

Write down that next actionable step and begin to plan out steps you could follow from there to eventually eliminate it entirely. There's no need to be exhaustive yet. The point is that simply seeing a plan can help remove the stress—while also providing a clearer path forward to a performance that can remove that issue in time.

CHAPTER 2

An Eye for Goal

It's in the early days of the 2001–2002 season, and Manchester United faces a tricky fixture. They're on a bad run of away form, winning only one of their last fourteen. In the first half, the game goes about as poorly as it could. By the halftime whistle, United is down 3-0.

According to Andy Cole, the gaffer gave the team a unique halftime talk in an effort to inspire a comeback. As he would later recall to manutd.com, "I remember the manager not saying a word for fifteen minutes." It was only in the last seconds of halftime that he spoke. "Once the bell went, [Sir Alex] said, 'Okay, you'd better go out there and win the game.'"[1]

That certainly did the trick. Simply speaking the possibility of victory reenergized the team. Cole went on to score in the first minutes of the second half, and goal after goal rained in from then on. By the final whistle, the scoreboard recorded an incredible comeback: 3-5 United.

---

1   Adam Marshall, "Countdown to 2018/19: Cole's Verdict on Our Rivals," Manchester United, June 13, 2018, https://www.manutd.com/en/news/detail/andy-cole-discusses-united-big-rivals-ahead-of-fixture-release.

Making Sure Your Shots Are on Target

It's amazing what clear goals can do for you. Whether it's mounting an almost unbelievable comeback or hitting a new sales record, having the correct destination in mind is a huge part of getting there.

The opposite is also true. If you don't know where you want to go, you can end up putting a lot of effort into going in the wrong direction. After all, no one cares how hard a player was working if the end result is an own goal.

This is why we have to begin any advice on planning with a discussion on goal setting. To avoid wasting your time on own goals, there's a simple process you can use to figure out where you want to go and the steps necessary to get there. All you have to do is visualize aspirational goals, define three-year goals, and plan how you're going to move toward them each day. With that in place, it becomes far easier to start making progress every day.

VISUALIZE

What would your life look like if you could wave a magic wand and have whatever you wanted? No restrictions, no limitations: What would your perfect life look like?

I like to think of this as a "what if" exercise. "What if I could retire at fifty?" "What if I could buy that beach house?" "What if I could start my own company?" "What if I could have that big family?"

Thinking like this can feel unnatural sometimes. It can seem childish. Why waste time daydreaming?

But there's evidence that visualizing helps your brain subconsciously seek out ways to achieve what you want. Think about when you're in a busy café. There's chitter-chatter in every direction. For the most part, you only notice this as background noise—until you hear someone call out your name. All of a sudden, you perk up immediately and seek out where that specific noise came from.

Have you ever noticed how good your brain is at figuring out the direction that voice came from? You might hear your name only once, but you can generally pinpoint where the person is just from that. Your brain is conditioned to seek out the specific sound of your name through all that noise.

Soccer players have been using visualization techniques for generations. Wayne Rooney used to use an old Pelé trick to get the upper hand before a game. He'd ask the kit man the day before the match what color United and the opposition would be playing in. That night, he'd go home and visualize tearing the defense apart—in detail, using the colors he knew both teams would be wearing. The exercise clearly worked for him.

Your brain can do the same thing with opportunities to lead you toward your goals—if you give it clarity on the direction you want to go.

This might all still feel a little vague, so let's imagine you're setting up your ideal life as your starting eleven. We'll play a straightforward 4-3-3 here.

The Ultimate Goal
4-3-3

Up front, you've got your forward line: your physical, mental, and emotional goals. This is what you want for your body and your mind. Behind your forward, you have a midfield covering the most important aspects of your life: your personal, friendship, and family goals.

Now let's get a bit more defensive. Let's consider the things that give you a foundation and stability. That's what you want in your professional, spiritual, community, and financial life.

In goal, we'll put your recreational goals.

You want clarity on all these areas so you can point them toward your ultimate goal: the life you want to lead.

Here's what my most recent 4-3-3 looked like:

- Physical goals: I've completed an Ironman triathlon.

- Mental goals: I am fluent in Arabic. I read twice daily. I write daily.

- Emotional goals: I meditate daily.

- Personal goals: I am a bestselling author.

- Friend goals: My friends and I continue to meet up twice a year. We never break that commitment.

- Family goals: Everyone loves each other, and we all live in the same town.

- Professional goals: I'm a TED speaker. I'm on the board of a professional soccer club.

- Spiritual goals: I feel content and purposeful in life.

- Community goals: I'm on the board of US Soccer.

- Financial goals: I am debt-free. I have saved enough to retire whenever I want.

- Recreational goals: My family and I continue to take vacations together.

Once you have this vision in place, let's do some work to shrink some of those dreams down to what you feel you could complete in these areas in three years' time.

Here are some of my three-year goals:

- Physical goals: I've completed that Ironman.

- Mental goals: I can speak *some* Arabic. I have read all the books on my bookshelf. I write daily.

- Emotional goals: I meditate four times a week.

- Personal goals: I have published my first book.

- Friend goals: I haven't broken the streak of meeting up with my friends twice a year.

- Family goals: We're all still living near each other. We still love each other.

- Professional goals: My company has been sold. I'm on the board of an MLS club. I'm an advisor on at least one start-up.

- Spiritual goals: I continue to feel content and sleep well at night.

- Community goals: I've made some inroads with US Soccer and have some role in the organization.

- Financial goals: All my commercial loans are paid off.

- Recreational goals: The family and I have enjoyed an amazing 2026 World Cup. We've visited Japan. We went on a safari. We've visited England.

PLAN

With a vision of where you want to go in place, all you have to do is plot the steps to get there. You can discover these steps simply by continuing to shrink the timeline on all of your goals. What do you need to do in the next year to be on track for each of your three-year goals? What do you have to do each quarter to hit those one-year targets? What about each month? And each week? And each day?

From here, I like to break things down further, into thirty- or even fifteen-minute blocks. However, if this feels too intense for you, you could simply list the daily goals or break them into morning, afternoon, and evening goals.

Aspirational goals

Three-year goals

Annual goals

Monthly goals

Weekly goals

Daily goals

Ninety-minute blocks

Thirty-minute blocks

Fifteen-minute blocks

Open space blocks

For those of you who feel ready to take your planning to the pro level, it's time for you to break out your weekly planner. This is the holy grail of your weekly actionable tasks and how we "get stuff done." I have included a download of my weekly planner at the link at the end of this chapter so you can print it and use it each week. I actually print fifty-two of them the first week of January so there is never an excuse to skip planning my week.

The weekly planner goes like this. On the left-hand column, list the areas in your life that you have responsibilities for and require action each week. Let's call these "roles." Make sure there are no more than seven roles—typically five is the norm. These should be both work and personal responsibilities, as the weekly planner ensures balance through your work/personal life. My current roles are:

1. XL Academy Winter Park

2. XL Academy Lake Nona

3. Author

4. Senior advisor

5. XL Corp.

6. Individual/personal

7. Family

Then I write the three tasks per role I need to achieve for the upcoming week based on my monthly goals. I take my time here. This is not a case of rushing to fill in the three tasks just to get it done. I typically do this Sunday late afternoon, so there are no time constraints on needing to get out of the house by a certain time.

Once this is filled out, next I:

1. Add into the daily section of the weekly planner the non-negotiable, time-sensitive appointments or commitments I

can't skip, such as preplanned meetings, appointments, and car pool commitments.

2. Add in my workouts for the week.

3. Set the twenty-one tasks (three for each of the seven roles) that I have committed to into time-specific blocks. Some of these will be ninety minutes, while others may only be fifteen- to thirty-minute tasks.

And there you have it. Your weekly planner is complete, and you are ready to smash your week. One thing you may notice once you're done is the amount of blank space in your weekly planner. That's good and essential. Remember, life rarely goes according to plan. One task may last longer than you thought, or you may have a "drop-in" from a client or friend. Those empty spaces provide the flexibility to move things around from time to time and still achieve your twenty-one tasks for the week.

However you break these down in your day, you're ready to get a planner and write out your tasks. This way you can build them into each day.

This is really only the beginning for improving your planning abilities, but it's the crucial first step.

PERFORM

We have a whole section ahead on performing, so I won't belabor this point here. Instead, here, I want to focus on the value of the plan as the key to preparing for performance.

Execution is often frustrating in soccer. A manager can only do so much. They choose the team, and they train the team. But once the game starts, it's on the players to perform. But there's still a lot that they can control. For instance, a manager can drill penalties. If the team practices them regularly, over and over again, they'll be prepared for them whenever the moment arrives.

That's your aim here: you want to create a situation in which the only option is to execute on your plan. The aim here, then, is to take away all your excuses so the only option is the hard work that leads to success.

Hard Work – Excuses = Success

"I don't know what I'm doing." Yes, you do. It's on your schedule.

"I don't have time." You do. You already budgeted it out.

"I don't know why I'm doing this." You do. It's leading you to accomplish all your life goals.

By having a plan written out and scheduled down to the half hour, you remind yourself what you have to do and why you're doing it. That makes it much easier to remain motivated and to complete the work consistently.

By using this method, you don't even need to remain motivated or remind yourself why you are doing it. You already did that in the planning; you just have to show up and do the work.

Game Time

It's time to write out your own 4-3-3 as you visualize your ideal future. As you do the visualization exercise, be sure to write everything down on a piece of paper. Use a pen. Writing things down makes them feel more real and more permanent.

At the top of the page, put your age and the date. Then put down every category you're filling in and start visualizing. Break these dream goals down into three-year goals, then one-year goals, and so on.

When you're done, buy a good planner and start filling tasks in to set you on the path to reaching those goals. Or you can download templates for planners and schedules at www.soccerofsuccess.com.

CHAPTER 3

The Big Three

I have no inner knowledge of the training Erling Haaland does every day to remain one of the best strikers in the world, but I'd be willing to bet good money that the vast bulk of his time is spent on three things: finishing, shooting, and heading. I doubt he ever practices throw-ins, and defense is most likely an afterthought.

I'd also bet his teammate, Ederson, spends almost all his time practicing shot stopping, passing out of the back, and driving the ball long up the pitch with accuracy. Does he ever practice headers on the off chance he's got to go into the opponent's box at the end of a game once a season? Does he spend much time dribbling around the middle of the pitch? I doubt it. That's not where he can make the most impact.

The same was almost certainly true for Manchester United as well when David Beckham was wearing the number seven shirt. It's hard to imagine that Ryan Giggs and Paul Scholes were practicing many free kicks in those seasons. Why bother? Becks had that skill wrapped up. He practiced the free kicks because that was the best way he could help the team win.

Every position on the pitch follows this principle. Each player has a different set of priorities and responsibilities. Some of those may overlap at times—a team may have two or three players who take free kicks, for instance—but the key is for each player to focus on being the best at the most important aspects of their role. And the same is true for you in your work, no matter what you do.

Missed Priorities

Just as a winger, a defender, a striker, and a keeper all have different roles and different responsibilities, so, too, does everyone in your life and organization. The CEO's priorities are different from those of the COO and the head of sales, which are different from team leaders, software developers, and HR professionals—and so on throughout the entire company. Your responsibilities within your family are different from those of your spouse, which are different from those of your children and your other relatives.

This is fairly obvious, but this basic fact often gets lost in the day-to-day work we do. Far too often, a manager ends up spending most of their time contributing to projects they were meant to only supervise. The CEO gets distracted by sales numbers; members of the tech department get pulled from their priority work to handle another department's needs.

And that is all the more common the smaller your organization. If you run your own company with fifteen employees, you're likely running from department to department all day, filling in everywhere there's a gap.

At the same time, family members often end up ignoring their responsibilities when life gets hectic, and we skip the things we intended to prioritize in our own lives—like our workouts or healthy eating routines.

In other words, if you don't plan a way to focus on your top priorities, it's almost inevitable that you'll get caught up in the day-to-day issues that come to a head across your life.

Even if you have structures in place to reduce this possibility, there are other risks you have to face. In particular, it's very easy to slide into the habit of doing the work you like instead of the work you should be doing.

If you've ever been promoted to leadership, you've probably experienced the difficulty of transitioning from *doing* to *managing*. Instead of working on projects directly, suddenly, you're supervising multiple projects without getting into the trenches. It's difficult to stop dabbling in that work and to focus on your new priorities. Instinctively, you want to return to the tasks you did well, the ones you understood thoroughly and were good at.

But in this case, your instincts are wrong. They pull you away from what you need to be doing. This can happen even when you intend to focus on what matters. When is the last time you had a priority that you kept putting off just because you didn't really want to do it? It was boring or a little outside your comfort zone, and so it just sat on your agenda for weeks on end. Maybe that was presenting a big idea in a meeting, or maybe it was committing to more structure and discipline with your kids.

Whether it's a lack of organization or a lack of willingness, this only holds you back. A soccer team can't win if everyone confuses their roles and refuses to do the tough work they like least. You can't win if your left back refuses to track back. That may be their least favorite part of the job, but it might be the most important.

That's why you need a system that allows you to plan to take on those crucial tasks even when it's far easier to ignore them.

Defining Your Big Three

Everyone falls into the trap now and again of wasting an hour of their lives. They stay after lunch to indulge in work gossip. They skip a workout to enjoy a lie-in. Or they eat that delicious burger even though it'll shatter the diet they're on. The difference between successful people and the also-rans is that successful people are quick to get back on track. They identify their mistakes and immediately get back to working on their priorities.

To do this, though, you have to know what those priorities are. We've already started defining those through your goals. With the insights from chapter 2, you should now have a set of tasks you need to accomplish every day. But life is busy, and most of us fall behind on our responsibilities from time to time. We get distracted or put things off for all the reasons I laid out previously.

For this reason, it's important to know all responsibilities that you really should focus your attention on, no matter how distracted you get in other areas of your life. I call those responsibilities your Big Three. Your Big Three includes the three tasks that are most impactful in your efforts to succeed and achieve your goals.

The Big Three for a striker is working on heading, shooting, and finishing, just like Erling Haaland. The Big Three for the salesperson is working on their sales pitch, making calls to clients, and following up to close deals. For a parent, it might be preparing healthy meals, helping their kid with homework, and maintaining family rules and discipline. In every aspect of life—whether in business, soccer, or life at home—everyone has a list of around three tasks that provide 90 percent of their contribution to their company, team, or family.

Your aim should be to discover what those three are for you.

Over the last year, much of my focus has been on getting my school, XL Academy, off the ground. For that reason, my Big Three tasks have been:

- Getting the school ready for an accreditation visit

- Closing sales for the school

- Completing all the permitting applications for the school

Those are not my favorite parts of my job. They all involve a lot of paperwork and mundane tasks that I'd rather put off. But they also happened to be the most important responsibilities I had on my desk. Completing those three tasks would do the most good for my company. They would make the biggest impact on our efforts to launch XL Academy. For a time, filling out that paperwork was my David Beckham free-kick practice.

But if I didn't have them listed and laid out clearly, I likely would have neglected them more often than not. It's only once I set those priorities down on paper—in a place where I could refer to them often and easily—that I was able to prioritize my time around accomplishing them.

Reexamine Your Big Three

As players evolve in their careers, they sometimes change roles. And in changing their roles, they have to adjust their Big Three priorities. A young winger may move into the number nine position. That would mean their previous priority of sprinting down the wings and crossing the ball gets replaced by a priority to get in the box, chest down those crosses, and knock them into the back of the net.

This transition was central to Robbie Mustoe's career. While many of you may know him as a wise and entertaining presence on NBC these days, Mustoe really made his name in the sport as an attacking midfielder for Middlesbrough. When Boro got promoted to the Premier League, though, the team brought in two new players, Juninho and Emerson—both attacking midfielders. Mustoe could have kept his head down and hoped for an opportunity back into the squad. Instead, he realized the best contribution he could make to the team was as a defensive midfielder. He recalibrated and focused on his tackling, passing, and positional awareness.

He'd eventually go on to be named the team's player of the season in 1999.

The same potential is present in your life. You will regularly find that your Big Three changes, whether that's because a project ends or because you take on a new role. As you move forward, don't just check off items on your Big Three list—replace them.

After my school got accredited, I replaced that Big Three responsibility with one focused on management. That was my next most impactful task. When your children graduate from high school, that will leave a big gap in your Big Three. Make sure you switch out that no-longer-useful task with the one that is now most important.

That doesn't mean you should always change out your Big Three, particularly when the urge to make the change comes from struggling to complete a task. At one point, David Beckham was the most hated man in England following his red card against Argentina in the 1998 World Cup. But as a true professional, he apologized, refocused, and got back to work like a true winner. Fast-forward to 2001, and Becks scored the free kick that sent England to the 2002 World Cup.

Suddenly, he was the most loved man in England—all because he stuck with his Big Three and continued to develop that marvelous free kick of his.

Whether changing out a priority or not, the value here is to focus on what you can do to best help achieve your goals. As long as you keep focused on that, the results will come.

Game Time

Lay out your current Big Threes. On a piece of paper, write "Work" and "Home" like the example below. These are the three priorities at work and home that can have the most impact in your professional and personal life that only you can do. They can't be easily delegated. Remember, your Big Three will constantly change over time as you complete big projects, but it's where you want to spend 90 percent of your time. Spoiler alert: email is not one of your Big Three!

Work

   1.

   2.

   3.

Home

   1.

   2.

   3.

CHAPTER 4

Prioritize Your Energy

James Milner is a real testament to the value of hard work. He's had an incredible career playing for some of the biggest clubs in England. He went from Leeds to Newcastle to Aston Villa to Manchester City to Liverpool and finally to Brighton & Hove Albion. Undeniably, he's a talented player, but the quality that everyone always brings up about him is the hard work he puts in. He's been an incredibly reliable hard worker for decades now.

I recently heard him on a podcast speak about the challenge of keeping up that legendary work ethic. The podcaster asked him about those times when he wasn't being picked to start each week. Did he ever fall into a negative mindset and find himself working a little less hard? After all, it's so much easier to go for a night out, to start eating badly, to start training a little less intensely—especially when you aren't getting the results you want from all those sacrifices.

Milner's answer was an emphatic no. What makes Milner different is that such setbacks make him work harder, not give up. He trains harder and makes his place on the team sheet undeniable.

Milner doesn't necessarily have more energy than any other players; he simply prioritizes how he builds up that energy and how he spends it. Instead of going out, he gets a good night's sleep. That allows him to get to training on time every day, ready to show what he can do. He puts the right things into his body, takes care of himself, and creates the circumstances where he can prove his reliability.

These choices have knock-on effects. A bad habit may not punish you the first time or even the thirtieth time you indulge, but over time, it will affect how well you succeed.

To see that, there are an unfortunately large number of examples of players who let their bad habits get the best of them. Perhaps the most obvious is Paul Gascoigne, or Gazza as we all know him. He was a truly incredible player, a momentous talent. But his addiction issues and poor discipline destroyed his career. Famously, after helping England secure a place in the 1998 World Cup, Gazza was photographed out eating kebabs. It ended his international career. It was one bad decision too many, and the consequence was devastating.

I don't think even James Milner would say he's close to the natural talent of someone like Gazza. But he's had a better career because he managed his time and his energy far better. He took care of the things that mattered, and that put him in a position to keep performing into his late thirties.

Building Energy

Being disciplined like Milner requires you to be disciplined about how you spend your energy—and that requires you to be disciplined about how you plan your time. Time management isn't just about your Big Three or checking off tasks to achieve your goals. You won't be able to do that if you lack the energy and focus to do the work. Any parent of a newborn knows the struggle of just getting through the day. The exhaustion is so intense that it's difficult to concentrate on anything. When we miss out on sleep, we reduce how well we can perform in that big meeting or how charming we are with that new client.

That means you need to build your days around filling up your energy reserves so you can perform better across a longer period of time. If you deplete yourself regularly, you'll feel the pain sooner or later, and all those tasks will go uncompleted.

Luckily, the list of things you need to do to build that energy is not long. The key areas where you can build energy are as follows:

- A great night's sleep

- A clear head

- A good diet

- A consistent exercise routine

These four requirements are foundational for any success, and we should aim to achieve them each day. If you sleep well; avoid a heavy head from drinking, too much screen time, and other bad habits; eat well; and get in a good workout, you can make sure you are set up to have a great day each day. And if you plan to do all these in the morning, as I do, you can guarantee a great day by lunchtime.

That doesn't mean challenging issues won't arise, but if they do, you'll be in the best mental and physical space to deal with them.

Think about how great professional players must feel after a tough training session when they come in with a clear head, a full belly from a nutritious breakfast, and the energy that comes after a great night's sleep. After they shower and hit the tactical room, that Champions League fixture against Real Madrid in two days no longer looks so tricky; it now feels downright winnable. Compare that to the player who went out the night before, got in at 2:00 a.m. after a few too many, slept terribly, and ate too much late-night pizza. After dragging themselves through practice—if they show up at all—they can't wait to get home. Everything feels overwhelming, let alone playing one of the giants of Europe.

The same is true in your own life. Talking with an angry client, heading a big presentation, or grinding through some complex data analyses are all easier to manage when you're well rested, clearheaded, and energized. It's easier to clean the house, work through the drama of your child's teenage heartbreak, and cook a great dinner when you are fortified with more energy.

These results build over time. If you prioritize these four areas five times in a row, you'll guarantee you'll have a great week. Maintain that for four weeks straight, and you'll have a great month. The longer you maintain this schedule, the more you can achieve.

These ideas are so powerful that Jeff Bezos himself endorses them. Even with all his peers following the Silicon Valley mindset of working 24-7, he said that he would consider it an injustice to his shareholders not to get eight hours of sleep each night. Bezos feels these areas contribute to his ability to succeed at one of the largest companies on earth.[2]

They can do the same for you.

Schedule Your Energy

Hitting all four of these targets seems simple on the surface, but in reality, it requires a lot of planning. We all know how easy it is to

---

2   Sean Wolfe, "Jeff Bezos Explains Why He Thinks Getting 8 Hours of Sleep Is Key to Making Important Decisions in the Workplace," *Business Insider*, September 14, 2018, https://www.businessinsider.com/ jeff-bezos-why-8-hours-sleep-important-when-making-important-decisions-2018-9.

stay up later than we intended, to skip that morning jog, or to order DoorDash after a long day. We're all tempted to watch more television than is really good for us or to stay out and have a few more drinks than we ought to.

The great news here is that these actions are all completely under your control. You can choose to skip happy hour. You can decide to drink green tea over wine after dinner. You can limit your TV intake to an hour or ninety minutes an evening. You can cook or order healthier meals. You can set your own bedtime. And you can get up earlier and get that workout in every morning.

That's not to say this is easy to fit into a busy day. You have social obligations, business responsibilities that can run later than expected, kids, a spouse, and who knows how much else to fit into your day. And that's before you set any time aside to relax. But there are some things you can do to accommodate the things that will replenish your energy.

You can start by building a "winding down" routine and a "getting up" routine. These are thirty- to sixty-minute periods before bed and after you wake up that can close out your days and start them back up successfully—the equivalent of warming up for a game and warming down afterward.

Set a time to begin your winding down routine each evening. During that period, turn down the lights, drink some herbal tea, turn off your devices, and do some light reading. Your getting-up routine should start with your alarm clock. If you have kids, you might want to try getting up a little before them. During this period, avoid phones and computers and focus on things that warm up your body and mind. I like to have some tea, journal, and do more of that light reading. I also do twenty-five push-ups, not as part of my workout but simply to wake up the body.

Once you build these schedules into your day, they can become automatic. And the more they become the standard instead of the exception, the easier it is to build those energy reserves over longer and longer periods.

Put Your Oxygen Mask On First

My friend, Joe Bradley, was the first person to employ me as a coach. He brought me over from England, and he helped get me started here. For obvious reasons, he's always been a mentor of mine.

I remember one time, many years back, when he left a powerful impression on me. I was just getting my first business up and running. Everything was hustle, hustle, hustle. I called Joe one day, and he told me that he only had a little time to chat. The reason was simple: at 2:00 p.m., he was going to the gym. He always went to the gym at that time. No exceptions. It didn't matter who he was talking to or what pressures he was under. That time was nonnegotiable.

I couldn't believe it. How could he have built up such a successful career when he took an hour out of his workday every day and went to the gym?

But his reasoning was sound. He knew that he performed better the rest of the day if he got that workout in at 2:00 p.m. He had to be selfish in order to be at his best.

It often takes that kind of selfishness to fit in all the activities you need to perform. It's a necessary counter to the selflessness that makes up much of your life. With family and business, you want to be of service to people. That means you often put your own needs last. And what are the areas of your life you can abandon easiest? Those energy-filling activities like sleep, working out, and healthy eating. But giving these things up just depletes you. It leaves you with less energy for the day. Over time, it leaves you with less energy across your whole life.

The fitter you are, the better you perform, and to stay fit, you have to put your fitness first. That level of fitness only has to increase the more successful you become. The higher a player moves up the ranks of the soccer leagues, the fitter they need to be. It doesn't matter how great their touch is; nobody is going to sign them if they are huffing and puffing around the field after fifteen minutes.

This same principle is true across your life. You won't be able to be a great romantic partner, manager, entrepreneur, or volunteer if you lack the energy to perform at the level required. Planning for time to reenergize gives you the endurance to focus and perform in all the areas it matters.

It's like the advice they give you on airplanes. You put your oxygen mask on first before you put one on your child. It does no one any good if you pass out before you can get the mask on either of you. It's for their benefit that you put yourself first in that case. It's the same here. Give yourself the chance to be healthy and clear thinking, and you'll do more to benefit everyone else.

The Right Kind of Selfishness

Why are strikers the most valuable players in the world? Their talent, of course. But to unleash that talent requires a certain kind of selfishness. They have to take shots other players would get shouted at for. They have to demand the ball every time it reaches the final third. They have to put their goal tally above almost every other consideration.

This selfishness is valuable. It helps the team. Of course, it's possible to be too selfish as a striker. You can refuse to pass when another player is open. You can moan over a foul for so long you take yourself out of the game. You can refuse to defend when the team needs you in the opposition box.

The same is true here. You need to be selfish about taking care of your energy and your health. But that's not an excuse to be selfish in everything. Being selfish isn't about giving yourself whatever you want. It's about taking care of yourself so you can do all the stuff that matters.

Taking an hour to work out has value for everyone. Taking an hour every day to have a few drinks is less valuable. That's not to say you shouldn't ever have those drinks. Seeing friends can be energizing. It's important to plan times to enjoy yourself. But that shouldn't have the nonnegotiable top-priority status of those routines that regularly build your energy. This is meant to be the tough medicine that keeps you healthy, not the fun stuff you spend some of that energy on.

> **1 hour of pain = 23 hours of pleasure**
> **1 hour of pleasure = 23 hours of pain**

You're making time for this because it helps you perform better. The other stuff is valuable—and you need to fit it in—but it's a net spend on your energy. And prioritizing it over everything else makes you the wrong kind of selfish.

Let's put it this way: it's not the sort of thing you'd ever catch James Milner doing.

Game Time

List your winding-down (ninety minutes before lights out) and getting-up routines here. I have listed mine as an example:

Getting-up routine:

1. Twenty-five push-ups

2. Pint of water

3. Prepare pu-erh tea

4. Journal while drinking tea

5. Read

6. First MIT of the day

Winding-down routine

1. Hot shower

2. Prepare tea

3. Evening journal

4. Phone on airplane mode

5. Read

6. Lights out

CHAPTER 5

The Ninety-Minute Mindset

I work with the former Premier League player Alan Smith. He's the loveliest, kindest, sweetest guy you'll ever meet—most of the time. You see, Alan's also on my amateur soccer team, and when the whistle blows, something changes in him. He transforms from this sweet guy into a real warrior. He's ultracompetitive. Nothing matters but winning.

That intensity is what he was famous for as a player. He came up through Leeds, where a tackle is celebrated more than a goal. He exemplifies the attitude that concept represents. He would press, tackle, and close down anyone in an effort to get the ball back and turn that possession into a chance. As Alan recently told me, "In training I would tell myself I'm the worst player in the world, and in games that I am the best player in the world."

At any other time, Alan can be charming, easy-going, and relaxed. But he's always known when it was time to give his all. And that allowed him to build a storied career at some of the top clubs in the world.

Very few of us can ever muster the level of intensity Alan brings to ninety minutes of soccer, but that doesn't mean we can't learn from him. If we set aside ninety minutes to demand the most of ourselves, we, too, can accomplish some pretty incredible things.

Setting Up Your Ninety-Minute Focus

With your schedule taking shape, you should now have time to get yourself up in the morning and wind yourself down at night, while making sure you get enough sleep and start each day with exercise, a good meal, and a clear head. You also have a list of things you have to get done each day to build toward your ultimate goals and your Big Three priorities where you make the most impact in work and life.

At this point, the most valuable tool you're missing is focus. You need to plan time to set aside to really focus on the work that matters so you ensure it doesn't get lost in your busy days. Far too often, we take on tasks as they come to us, and by the time we get around to the important stuff that would allow us to move toward our goals, we've simply run out of time and energy—even when we start the day strong.

The problem is that most of us are so easily distracted. We have our phones. We have relationships that introduce drama throughout our day. New demands are made on us at work. Even if we're primed to do our best, we don't get the chance to perform.

One of the great things about soccer—and sports in general—is that it cuts through all these distractions. For the entire time the team is on the pitch, they're focused. There are no phones, no girlfriends or boyfriends, no email, no paperwork. For ninety minutes, the players get to focus solely on performing.

We may not all be professional athletes, but we can create the same structure in our own lives. We can set up ninety-minute sessions each day to focus on what really matters. We can create a time in our schedule to summon our inner Alan Smith and go all out to get it all done.

Just like the pros, we can break this time down into chunks: forty-five minutes for performance, a short fifteen-minute break to recover, and then forty-five more minutes of focused work. During these periods, we can marshal all our resources, remove all distractions, put our most important work in front of us, and give it our all. I've included examples of everyday and pro schedules here for reference.

PRO	BEGINNER
Wake up	Wake up
Drink water	Read
Meditate	Excercise
Journal	Recover
Read	45-min. block
45-min. block	Recover
Exercise	45-min. block
Ice bath	Lunch
Recover (shower and smoothie)	45-min. block
45-min. block	Recover
Recover	45-min. block
45-min. block	Recover
Lunch	15-30 min. blocks for remainder of work day
45-min. block	
Recover	
45-min. block	
Recover	
15-30 min. blocks for remainder of work day	

I can't claim to have invented this idea myself. It's an extension of the well-known Pomodoro Technique. But the periods of concentration in the Pomodoro Technique tend to be shorter—around twenty-five minutes each time. Here, you have more time in each focused period, allowing you to get far more done while maintaining that high level of focus.

Just like your get-up and wind-down schedules, this should be a nonnegotiable part of your day, protected from all interference. I like to put my phone on airplane mode, so I don't receive messages or emails. I can use the phone for a resource, but it can't distract me.

As for when you schedule your ninety minutes, ideally, it should be the first thing you do at work. If you've warmed up your brain well by prioritizing your energy, you'll be ready to jump into this right away.

On particularly busy days, you can even add a second ninety to the second half of your day to cover the overflow. Like playing two or three games in a week, that's going to put more strain on you, but when required, you can plan to perform twice.

Choosing Your Tasks

But what tasks should you fill your ninety-minute sessions with? In a word, frogs.

Brian Tracy wrote an excellent book called *Eat That Frog!* The lesson within it was simple. It's based on a line from Mark Twain. If you had to eat a frog every day, the great writer suggested, the best way to go about it would be to eat it first thing in the morning.

According to Tracy, we all have frogs we have to eat each day, but our instinct is often to put it off as long as possible. We hate working out. We hate doing paperwork. We hate making sales calls or letting someone go.

Whatever it is, there's something that we have to do that we really don't want to.

So we should follow Twain's advice and simply get it out of the way first. Look back at your Big Three. These are the most important tasks you have, even if they aren't your favorite. Start your ninety by tackling the parts of your Big Three that you least like doing. You can also add in here tasks related to your goals that you'd rather put off. If you really hate cleaning your house, break some big chores up into forty-five-minute sessions, and finish them early. If you really don't like filling out forms or reviewing statistics, do it first thing so you don't have to worry about it for the rest of the day.

Importantly, while any type of task can fit into your ninety minutes, you should focus on a small number of tasks in each ninety—ideally either one split across two forty-five-minute periods or two forty-five-minute tasks.

For smaller frogs, leave those to the "open spaces" you find in your schedule throughout the day. Open spaces are small gaps that appear in your schedule. Those are the perfect opportunities to complete a five-minute task like writing an email, paying a bill, or a quick bit of research on a potential client. These aren't the bigger frog tasks that require your ninety minutes of focus. Those sessions should be for the tasks that require you to really step up and perform.

Organizing your time this way can help reduce stress, free up time, and keep your mind clear for everything else that's ahead in the day.

As for those occasional second nineties, I tend to think it's better to focus on "reactive" tasks there. Most people aren't as sharp in the second half of the day as they were in the beginning, so it's better to turn the afternoon focus periods into work related to responding to the needs others have put on you. Answer those emails or provide that feedback. I always schedule a single forty-five-minute block for checking email each day. Sometimes, I add another block if I'm engaged in an email-heavy project. Whether you place email responsibilities here or not, though, this should be lighter work that still has a high priority, so that when you're done you have tasks cleared and enough energy to see out the rest of the day.

Don't Forget the Warm Down

After a game, every player needs a good warm down. This includes some stretching and light exercise to help the muscles recover from all that exertion. We'll dig into these warm-down activities and what they can teach us in the rest/review part of the book. For now, though, let's focus on warming down during and after those ninety-minute sessions you've scheduled into your day.

After each forty-five-minute focus session—and after a completed ninety—you need the same kind of active break that players require. Get up and move. Get your brain away from work, if only for a few minutes to reset. Otherwise, the alternative is sitting yourself to death with no break to stretch your legs and rest your mind.

This is a good moment to get up and refill that water bottle. I always recommend drinking loads of water all day. Not only is this healthier than every other drink you can consume, but it also forces you to get up at moments like this to refill the bottle or head to the bathroom.

Once you've moved your body a bit, you can engage in some light, easy tasks before you get back to focused work. If there's a quick conversation you need to have with a coworker, get that in now. You want work that isn't creative or demanding. Avoid anything internet based so you don't get sucked into the dark cave of browsing or email distractions. That will allow your mind to recover before you hit the next session or move on to tasks at a more standard speed for the rest of the day.

Batching Tasks

The aim of your ninety-minute sessions is to focus on the work that really matters. And we can expand that mission beyond those focus periods to improve efficiencies throughout our day.

There are many activities that fill our day that we could either complete in a single session or else delegate to others.

One of the best ways to improve these efficiencies is through "batching." This is the process of bringing a set of activities together instead of doing them throughout the day. We all already batch certain activities naturally. Most of us do all of our daily bodily cleaning in the bathroom in one go. We shower and brush our teeth and comb our hair and put on deodorant. We do everything all at once because it is just much more efficient than coming back to the same room over and over to complete one task. When we do laundry, many of us do all the loads in a single afternoon. It's possible to do one load every day or two throughout the week, but we save time and focus by batching it all together.

We can use batching in our ninety-minute sessions as well. If you really have to do sales calls, batch them all together in that focus time so you can get it all done at once. Personally, I like to schedule all my meetings within a two-hour period to get that out of the way. Once again, you can do the same with emails. Batch them in your afternoon ninety and then avoid your inbox the rest of the day.

I've brought up email so many times here partly because it's easy to allow it to overwhelm your whole day, really crippling your performance. Just as a soccer player can experience "death by overtraining," a professional can experience "death by too much emailing/texting."

Email and text can be major threats to our focus throughout the day. A study from Microsoft found that it takes around twenty-five minutes to refocus on a task after we respond to an email.[3] If you get a text or check an email four times a day, you're potentially losing more than two hours of work. That's more than ten hours a week. Freeing yourself from receiving messages in your ninety-minute focus periods and bundling your conversations at other times of the day can save huge amounts of time.

If you tend to get distracted when checking social media, try to batch your usage into one period in the day. You can check after work from six to seven, for instance. That way, you catch up on everything happening without feeling the need to check every five minutes. By batching it in this way, you may also realize just what a waste of time social media can be.

Imagine how inefficient it would be for a professional soccer player to go outside every five minutes and sign five autographs. It would take all day! We'd laugh at how ridiculous that was and suggest they just stay out there for twenty minutes to sign all of them in one chunk. Yet we can be guilty of doing just that by constantly checking texts, emails, and social media every five minutes.

I like to batch my food prep for the week. Instead of taking fifteen minutes to prep my lunch every morning, I spend thirty minutes

---

3   Aaron Taube, "You Lose Up to 25 Minutes Every Time You Respond to an Email," *Business Insider*, December 9, 2014, https://www.businessinsider.com/you-lose-up-to-25-minutes-every-time-you-respond-to-an-email-2014-12.

prepping all my lunches on Sunday. That frees up more time each morning to get the day up and running.

Obviously, this kind of work requires some discipline, and it may take time to adjust—but the value is there.

Is This Really Worth Your Time?

Batching isn't the only way to improve efficiency. You can also delegate where possible. The manager of a big club doesn't do all the work coaching their team by themselves. They'll have a set-piece coach focused on defending set pieces and scoring them. They'll have a goalkeeper coach. They'll have a first team coach and a youth coach. And that's really just the tip of the iceberg. Delegating responsibilities across the staff allows the manager to focus on picking teams, training, and winning games.

Delegation can be just as helpful in your life. I used to spend hours on QuickBooks. At some point, I asked myself: Is this really one of my Big Three tasks? Can someone else do this? Can I afford for them to do it? Can I be doing something more valuable with this time?

The answer was yes to all those questions. So I brought someone else in.

I do the same thing with a cleaner and a lawn care specialist. It used to take me four hours a week to handle all the outdoor work for our home. That was sixteen hours a month. It costs $120 a month to have someone else do it.

Is my time worth more than eight dollars an hour? Yes. So I outsourced it.

You don't have to be an expert in everything. In fact, that's a waste of your resources. Where you can hand off tasks to specialized experts, you'll get better results and free up more time to focus on the areas you make the biggest impact—such as on your Big Three or on time spent recovering and reviewing your progress.

Crossing the White Line

The key to the success of ninety-minute sessions is training yourself to hit the ground running as soon as the timer starts. For soccer players, this is like crossing the white line. Whether you're a starter or coming off the bench, as soon as you cross that line, you know it's go time. Players are ready to perform the instant they're on the pitch.

How do they get to that point? Part of it is a good warm-up, but a lot of it has simply become automatic. They've run onto the pitch so many times in their careers—not just in games but thousands and thousands of times on the training ground. They've done it so often that they've trained their bodies and minds to simply know what to do.

Your body and mind do the same thing. Think about how you act when certain events occur. When you step up to lead a meeting or make the call for a big sale or walk into the house to see the kids in the evening, your brain and your body know they have to be focused. It's automatic. When you get to church or walk into your boss's office, you know how you should act. You can train yourself to step up and perform in each of these circumstances.

The same can be true for your ninety-minute sessions. If you practice jumping into the work often enough, eventually, your body and mind simply know to hit the ground running when the time comes. And that allows you to expand these sessions or contract them as necessary.

If you follow this plan and "cross the white line" as soon as you start your ninety-minute sessions, you'll be prepared to cross it whenever the need arises. It's possible you'll have to run a seminar someday, which involves sessions that are usually forty-five minutes to an hour across an entire day. If you've automated your ability to cross the white line into hyperfocus, you can expand your ninety to accommodate this need. Just as players usually train for one game a week but can sometimes play three across seven days, you can expand to meet this need so long as you add more space to warm down and recover afterward.

You don't have to worry whether you'll show up. By then, it'll be automatic. And that's just the start of what automating can do for your planning and your performance.

Game Time

Start planning for the ninety-minute sessions that would make the most difference in your day.

At the same time, define your white line. Choose a trigger for immediately kicking on when you cross your white line. For me, it's a cup of pu-erh tea when I sit down to write, or my first cup of coffee for the day when I settle in for my first ninety minutes of the day. Some people choose the doorframe of the office they walk through before each forty-five-minute block. If you connect these triggers closely with your activities, your mind and body will come to associate the activity with productivity.

You might put on your workout gear right before warming up for a jog or choose a song you always play before walking into your first meeting in the morning. Whatever gets your mind and body ready to perform, harness it and turn that energy toward those activities that make you most productive.

CHAPTER 6

Automatic First Touch

Sometimes, in the midst of a game, you'll see a player display an incredible first touch. They'll bring down a ball flying across the pitch and control it instantly. With that single touch, they'll set themselves up perfectly for their second touch. It can seem so easy—if you've never tried to do it yourself. It's almost as if the ball goes wherever the player thinks to put it, no matter how it got to their foot.

But here's the thing: players rarely think about their first touch. They're thinking about what happens after it. The first touch itself is essentially automatic. The same is true for a great pass. They might intentionally pick out the pass, but they don't think about what their body has to do to complete it. Their body just knows.

The automatic ability to control the ball and place it where they want it frees them up to think about those big passes, clever nutmegs, and crucial runs. They can focus on dodging that two-footed tackle sliding their way (or making the most of the contact in front of the ref)—all because the technique that we all marvel at in the stands has been put on autopilot.

Autopilot Takes Practice

The value of autopilot within a game is obvious. When you don't have to think about the little things, you can focus on the big ones. When you're confident of your shooting form and the accuracy of your shot, you can focus on getting yourself in the best position for that shot. When you are hyperfit, you don't have to think or worry about fatigue setting in.

We use autopilot throughout our days for the same purpose. It frees up energy and focus for what matters. Your brain is like a cell phone battery. You charge it every night. With a full night's sleep and good evening and morning habits, you'll start the day with a full charge. But every mini decision you have to make drains some of that battery power. Putting certain things on autopilot saves your battery life, allowing you to use that energy where it can do the most good.

We don't tend to think much about how we brush our teeth or locking the door when we leave. We do those things automatically, and that preserves our focus for more important things.

But autopilot isn't always as easy to attain in more complex activities.

Great players have been able to put their first touch on autopilot because they've practiced it so many times before. This isn't something that develops after a few training sessions. We're talking about thousands of hours developing that level of skill.

Autopilot is a close cousin of mastery. While mastery is more nuanced, it does involve certain aspects of autopilot. A world-class violinist doesn't have to think where to put their fingers on the strings to produce the right notes. There's more to their skills than that autopilot, but the autopilot allows them to free their minds and focus on the qualities that produce a sound people will fill concert halls to hear.

A player can also master taking free kicks. There are crucial unique qualities in picking out the angles for each kick, but form and technique can be practiced to the point they're on autopilot—allowing the player to focus on those elements that will make all the difference.

I know that people associate mastery on this level with a certain number already: ten thousand. The idea is that if you spent ten thousand hours practicing something, you'll master it. And once you've mastered it, you've necessarily put certain aspects of that skill on autopilot.

The idea has some validity, but it isn't that simple. To truly master something, you can't just go through the motions. You have to practice the right way. And that means following our hat trick of success: plan, perform, recover with immediate feedback, and do the same thing all over again. You plan to practice particular elements of that activity, perform in a way that teaches your body or mind to do it right every time, and review to make sure you're meeting those standards.

A great soccer player has a great first touch because they planned and performed that specific action over and over again. They had coaches who reviewed what they were doing and helped improve form. Over and over, for thousands of hours—that's how you put complex acts on autopilot.

What Do You Want on Autopilot?

This begs the question, What should you aim to autopilot in your own life? To answer this, we need to ask a couple more questions: What activities do you put a lot of time into? Where could you most benefit from more autopilot?

Let's say you're in sales. If you make a lot of sales calls, it would really benefit you if you could have your pitch on autopilot. That would free you up to do all the other things that make a sale more likely: attentive listening, empathetic responses, and those little jokes that help win potential customers over. Since you have to make so many calls, the opportunity is there. Focus on improving the pitch, get feedback where you can, and over time, you'll find the pitch itself is on autopilot.

This same phenomenon is useful when having your response to customer complaints on autopilot, as well as your routine for getting up early, dealing with anger, or getting your kids ready for school.

Importantly, as you aim for new levels of autopilot, the goal here isn't to do these tasks mindlessly; it's to remove the number of tasks you have to consciously think about. If you're making a sales call with your pitch on autopilot, that doesn't mean you aren't paying attention while you're pitching. It means you don't have to worry about what you'll say next. You aren't zoning out; you're conserving energy. And that allows you to use it in more constructive ways. You can be present in the conversation because you know exactly what to say.

What Can You Put on Autopilot Today?

There's value in choosing what you want to master and put on autopilot, but that's also a huge investment that will take some time to pay off. So while you work on those complex automations, you can also look for areas in your life that you can already treat like your first touch.

To do this, think about the actions you have already "mastered" simply because they're part of your banal routines of existence. If you think about it, you likely already have tons of autopiloted routines when you get up, go to the office, leave the office, arrive back home, and go to bed. Further, if you've followed the advice of this book, you're already developing more effective practices here that you can soon put on autopilot. You won't have to think about buying the herbal tea or brewing it in the evening. You'll just do it.

From here, you can look for other daily activities that you can expand into autopilot. For instance, many successful people wear similar outfits every day. Steve Jobs made this famous with his iconic black turtlenecks. It's just one less decision he had to make. Or you could focus on meals. Create a meal schedule you follow each week. It can be the same lunch each day or the same seven dinners you cook Monday through Sunday. That will allow you to stop thinking about grocery lists and cooking.

Instead of putting your car keys wherever you think to put them down, put a hook on the wall and leave them there every time you come home. Now you'll never lose them again. You can expand this even further. I've been a runner for most of my life, so I don't really need to think about my form when I head out for a jog. I know the technique required. That allows me to clear my mind and replenish my mental energy while I'm getting exercise.

These may or may not all apply to you. If you're new to working out, you don't want to put exercise on autopilot. You may love variety in your food, so you want to keep changing up the menu. Maybe you're a fashionista, and your outfits really express who you are.

You can find your own way here, but the more you can consciously decide to put on autopilot, the more space you have open for everything else in your life.

One thing you can definitely start to put on autopilot, though, is your daily and weekly reviews for your goals. Set a time when you do them, and it will become automatic. More on this in part III.

When to Cancel Autopilot

The great thing about autopilot is that you can always cancel it. A pilot might not have to do most of the flying while the plane is in the air, but if there's an issue, they can always take control.

The same is true for soccer players. They may not usually think about that first touch, but they may choose moments to cancel the autopilot if necessary. In a close game, marked by three defenders, they may turn off the autopilot to really consider how they're going to control the ball when it comes to them. The same is true in certain key moments, such as when taking a penalty. That's a good time to focus on form and consciously deciding where you want to place the ball.

This applies to life as well. You don't think about brushing your teeth, unless your dentist tells you that you need to do it differently. You may not need to think about your sales pitch—unless it's a very important client with a unique set of requirements. Wearing the same outfits can be great, except when you're going on that big first date with someone you're really interested in.

Creating autopilot settings is about increasing your control over your life and increasing your energy reserves. You can decide when it's best to refocus on the action in front of you.

Turn Your Focus to Performance

Not every first touch turns into a great opportunity. Defenders slide in and take the ball; a teammate misses the pass you set up; a sloppy second touch goes out of bounds. No matter how much you put on autopilot or how well you plan, there are still issues that will crop up in the actual performance that you have to deal with.

That's why planning is only the first part of the hat trick of success. Once you've planned everything out to create the best possible opportunities, the next thing you have to do is actually get out there and perform.

Game Time

Think through your daily and weekly routines. What can you put on autopilot?

Can you put portions of your wake-up routine on autopilot? What about your routine for leaving the house, arriving at work, leaving work, or arriving home? What about your bedtime routine?

Choose at least one routine and put it on autopilot for a week. See if you notice that you've freed up more energy and focus for elsewhere in your life.

PART II

Perform

CHAPTER 7

Playing to Win

There may be no "I" in "team," but there is one in "win"—and top players understand that. Top players don't play to compete. They play to win at every level—all the time. If you go down to any Premier League training ground and observe a training session, you'll be amazed at how intense the games are in training. There's nothing at stake. They're playing against their own team. And yet, every player gives their all. They're tackling hard, running hard, and performing at the top of their abilities. When they lose, they're genuinely gutted.

Even if you can't go watch professionals practice, you can still see this phenomenon in your community. You'll find the same thing in any park where kids are playing a scrappy game together. There's nothing at stake beyond the game itself, and yet, everyone is striving; every kid is desperate to win.

Even when there's no scoreboard, no trophy at the end of the match, and nothing but pride on the line, every minute matters because each player is keeping score. Let me repeat that. The reason the games are so intense is because every player is keeping score of the game and of their own performance within it. They're playing to win every second. It drives them.

Of course, most of us only have a limited amount of that deep sense of competition and drive. What separates those Premier League players from the rest of us—beyond talent—is how much relentless drive they possess. We may find losing very uncomfortable, but they can't stand it.

That drive to perform may in fact be a greater asset than talent in many cases. Talent doesn't always translate to performance. You can be talented and lazy. We can all name players who fit that description— and despite all the promise, their careers peter out sooner or later.

On the other hand, combining modest talent with an immense drive to win is a far greater recipe for sustained success. Given enough time and enough opportunities, it's the ability to consistently play to win that will make the most difference.

Learning to Perform

We only have so much control over the talent we're born with. If talent was something we could choose, many of us would already know the lessons of this book—because we'd have played a long, prestigious soccer career. Luckily, we have a bit more control over the drive we bring to our performance.

How do we build this drive? How do we put ourselves in the best possible position to perform no matter the level of our talent and no matter the stakes? How do we come in every day and push for success in our goals?

According to Chris McChesney in his wonderful book *The 4 Disciplines of Execution,* we can break this drive down into four characteristics. Every player on the pitch has four things in common:

1. They know the goal.

2. They know what to do to achieve the goal.

3. They know the score at all times.

4. They hold themselves accountable regularly and frequently for the results of their efforts.

The keen readers out there will notice that this is really a slight variation on the plan, perform, recover hat trick of success that is key to utilizing the Soccer of Success. For instance, the value of planning can be seen in points one and two. In other words, we plan by knowing where we're going and what we need to do to get there. We perform by keeping track of the score. And holding ourselves accountable is central to review/recover. Here, though, we want to bring all these elements together within our performance in each game and through-out each season—or each day, month, and year at work and at home.

We enter performance enhanced by the planning that has brought us clarity of our goals. Success in soccer requires every player to know the goal for the season. But it also requires them to know the goal for each particular game. They should even break this down further and know their individual goal within each set-piece play. In short, they have to know what they're trying to achieve on every front from the smallest timeline to the longest.

If you've finished the first part of this book already, you should be able to implement all of this in your own life. You have the goals set, and you've worked them backward to show how performance each day can lead to the results you most want to see in your life. You also have the systems you can put in place to prioritize your most important responsibilities. You have a plan to prioritize your energy so you have enough fuel in the tank to do everything you need to do. You have a framework to block off time to get difficult work done.

And you have the means to automate tasks so you can bring your full attention to the activities that really matter.

In other words, you've set yourself up with clear goals, and you know what you need to do to achieve them. As you move directly into performance, these tools will continue to be an asset, allowing you to focus on points three and four in McChesney's system.

Keeping Score

With a plan firmly in place, we can start to build the scoreboard that will allow us to keep track of our progress toward the goals we already set. You know what you're performing for and how to perform. Now it's time to lace up your boots and get out on the field—while always keeping an eye on that scoreboard.

As I've already laid out, players are constantly keeping score. They're keeping score in the games on Saturday when the enormous scoreboards are impossible to miss. They're keeping score in training the rest of the week. They're also keeping score across the season. Though they may sometimes pretend otherwise, the Premier League table is in front of every player and coach before each game of the season. In other words, at all times, players are keeping score, and they are driven by it.

But they do more than just keep an eye on the scoreboard and league table. To ensure they remain on track across a season, they focus on metrics. They have key metrics they have to meet on a daily and weekly basis—and they know that by meeting those metrics, they prepare themselves for long-term success. They know when you add up all those focused training sessions, along with all those good nutritional choices and social sacrifices, the compound result will be a crack at a trophy or a chance to avoid relegation to stay in the league.

If you want to perform in your own life, you have to replicate this same mindset and structure. Keeping score requires you to have a sense of your success across those same short and long timelines. To do this, I recommend you create a physical scoreboard tracking your most important numbers.

Monthly Scoreboard Sample

Day	Date	SCORE	Work Out	SCORE	Morning Pages	Morning reading	Evening reading	Daily Score	% Score	Words Written	Big 3 Hours Allocated
Friday	1-Mar	1	0	0	0	1		7	75%	0	2
Saturday	2-Mar	1	0	0	0	1	0			0	
Sunday	3-Mar	1	0	0	0	0	0				
Monday	4-Mar	1	Swam 94 laps	1	1	1	0	8	100%		3
Tuesday	5-Mar	1	Peloton + Run	1	1	1	0	8	100%	0	3
Wednesday	6-Mar	1	Swam 100 laps	1	1	1	1	8	100%	0	3
Thursday	7-Mar	1	Ran 12 miles	1	1	0	0	8	100%	0	1
Friday	8-Mar	1	BAY HILL	0	0	1	0			0	
Saturday	9-Mar			0	0	0	0				
Sunday	10-Mar	1	56 Mile Bike	1	0	0	0				
Monday	11-Mar	1	100 Laps	1	0	0	0	8	85%		3
Tuesday	12-Mar	1	5 mile run	1	1	1	0	8.5	50%	0	2
Wednesday	13-Mar	1	122 Laps	1	1	0	0	7.5	85%		2
Thursday	14-Mar	1	Ran 12 miles	1	1	0	0	8	85%		3
Friday	15-Mar	1	Swam 80 laps + 2 hr bike	1	0	1	0	8	85%		2
Saturday	16-Mar	1	Cruise	0	0	0	0				
Sunday	17-Mar	1	Cruise	0	0	0	0				
Monday	18-Mar	1	40 min treadmill	1	0	0	0				
Tuesday	19-Mar	1	Cruise	0	0	0	0				
Wednesday	20-Mar	1	Weights	1	0	0	0				
Thursday	21-Mar	1	Cruise	0	0	0	0				
Friday	22-Mar	1	Disney 5k	1	0	0	0				
Saturday	23-Mar	1		0	0	0	0				
Sunday	24-Mar	1	Peloton + Run	1	0	0	0				
Monday	25-Mar	1	100 laps	1	0	1	0	7.5	85%	0	3
Tuesday	26-Mar	1	Peloton + Run	1	0	1	0	8	100%	0	3
Wednesday	27-Mar	1	126 laps	1	0	1	0	7	100%	0	2
Thursday	28-Mar	1	Ran 13.1 miles	1	0	1	0	8	75%	0	2
Friday	29-Mar	1	Swim 82 laps + 27 mile bike	1	0	1	0	7	75%	0	2
Saturday	30-Mar	1		0	0	0	0				
Sunday	31-Mar	1	52 mile tour de cure	1	0	0	0				
SCORE		100%		65%	19%	42%	3%	8	87%	0	

A scoreboard can be as simple as a page out of your daily planner with all the tasks you intend to complete on it. Cross out each task as you go through the day, and you'll always know the score. Or you could create a master spreadsheet that lays out the key tasks you want to focus on and a space where you can calculate how much you've accomplished throughout each day. An example can be found at the link at the end of this chapter.

However you construct it, you can use this scoreboard to make sure you're making the progress you need to for success. For instance, instead of guessing whether you're hitting your average number of sales calls each day, get the scoreboard out and put a real number behind it. That way, you know whether you've hit that ten-call-a-day minimum or not. That makes it easier to drive yourself to success. If you're on nine calls on Wednesday, you can push yourself to hit the mark. There is no way you are leaving the office that day until you make call number ten.

That tenth call could be the one that guarantees the result you're looking for. Even if everyone else is leaving for happy hour, you can eliminate your excuses by looking at that scoreboard. If it doesn't show ten calls, you're staying behind for five extra minutes to make that final call.

You can even share this scoreboard with others. Let your spouse know you intend to go for a run five nights a week. Your spouse can help you keep track, reminding you what the score is on those evenings you'd rather stay in and lounge. If your team knows you always want to hit ten calls, they can push you and motivate you when your own drive is giving out.

You can post your scoreboard on your mirror in the bathroom, so you have to stare at it every day and look at the check marks on it. You can post it at your desk. One technique I use is to prefill my calendar with my ideal goals. So if I want to go a full month of working out every day, I print the month out and add a check mark to each day like it's already been done. That motivates me to live up to the expectation I've set for myself and avoid cheating for a day.

Holding Yourself Accountable

The true value of sharing your scoreboards is that it helps you hold yourself accountable. Accountability is a necessary component of performance. One of the reasons players feel compelled to perform at all times is the weight of accountability placed on them not just by themselves but by others. Players are in the public eye so much that they are accountable at all times. They are interviewed by the press constantly. With social media, they can be held accountable in a matter of seconds by millions of fans at any time, day or night. They are also held accountable by their peers in the locker room.

There is no stronger drive than the thought of letting someone down. And you can build that drive into your performance by allowing others to hold you accountable.

Sharing your scoreboard is a great start in this area, but you can take this further by introducing some review elements within your performance. Introduce a weekly review of your scoreboards in front of your team at work or your spouse at home, and suddenly, performance becomes a public measurement. Everyone knows what you are trying to achieve, and you have to face falling short in front of those you respect.

It's a lot easier to justify missing a run or skipping a call when you only have to defend yourself to yourself. It's much harder when you have to explain it to the world.

Put yourself under the stadium lights the same way players have to perform, and you'll find that you have more drive to execute when the going gets tough. If your output on the pitch isn't what it should be, then your "fans" will let you know about it. If you are not pulling your weight and are constantly falling short, then your team—in your personal life or in the office—can provide the pressure you need to turn things around.

Plan Like a Bee, Train Like a Horse

For a long time, scientists were puzzled by the fact that bees could fly. They're too heavy; the proportions are all wrong. And yet somehow those bees stayed airborne. It shouldn't work, but it does.

When we make our plans, we should think like bees. The goals you set at the beginning of the first part of this book should start out free of restrictions and conditions. You're a bee, and you're aiming to fly. You'll figure out how later. The rest of Part I helped us reverse engineer your flight so you could figure out how to actually get off the ground.

Now, it's time to truly take off. As you prepare to fly, though, I want you to have a different animal in mind: the racehorse. Racehorses always show up to train and perform. They don't care what the weather is like or how they feel. Every morning, they go out and train. They stick to the plan. Whether they're hungry or tired or just having a bad day, it doesn't matter. Once they're out on the track, they run.

To reach your ambitious goals and truly fly against all odds, you've got to channel your inner racehorse for every performance. You have to look at that scoreboard and hit your targets no matter how you're feeling or what is going on in your life. You've made the plan; now stick to it.

Many young players are told they have the talent to make it as a pro. The ones who go from potential to professional are the ones who manage to consistently execute on the plan. They show up in training. They push in every practice game. They keep score, and they make sure they hit their targets.

Talent alone isn't enough. Performance is where you really determine whether you'll hit your goals or not. And that's true no matter what setbacks you encounter along the way.

Sir Richard Branson is dyslexic. He was told at a young age that he wouldn't amount to anything. Instead of giving up, he channeled his inner bee and planned for outrageous success. Then he acted like a racehorse and showed up every day, rain or shine, until he achieved it all. The combination of dreaming big and showing up allowed him to jump from creating hugely successful record stores to an airline and train services, and now he is aiming to send people to space.

In every moment, there is a hard decision and an easy decision—a right choice and a wrong choice. The best thing you can do to achieve what you want in life is to be a horse, put on your blinders, and keep making the tough, correct choices that drive the score up and make those impossible dreams slowly become possible.

> **Hard choices = Easy life**
> **Easy choices = Hard life**

At some point, this high-performance mindset can become intuitive. Being committed 99 percent of the time is brutal because you have to make thousands of decisions every day whether you're going to really do something or not. But if you're in 100 percent, you don't have to think about it. You just do it.

If you're going to play, you're playing to win.

Game Time

Set up your own scoreboard by downloading a template at www.soccerofsuccess.com.

CHAPTER 8

Practice Makes Permanent

We all know the value of practice. From an early age, almost every one of us was told that "practice makes perfect." But that's not quite right. Practice doesn't make perfect; it makes permanent. And that means you have to be careful what you are making permanent in your life.

In 1992, the back pass rule was introduced into the Laws of the Game. Before then, outfield players could pass the ball to their keeper, who could pick it up and throw it, drop it at their feet for a pass, or kick it up the field. This was a useful tactic in time wasting, so it was eliminated. From that point onward, a keeper could no longer pick up the ball if it had been kicked to them from someone on their own team.

That made sense moving forward, and I think the game is better for that change. But there was a price to be paid by the players who had developed some permanent muscle memory using the old rule. I remember the season following the rule change. Over and over again, Arsenal's keeper, David Seaman, kept picking up the ball when it was passed back to him by one of his teammates. Every time, it resulted in an indirect free kick in a dangerous area. But he couldn't stop doing it.

This wasn't down to any protest against the rules or purposeful decision. Seaman had simply practiced the old way of playing so much that it was second nature to him to pick the ball up. Practice had made that instinct permanent, and he couldn't just change it because the rules changed.

Through no fault of his own, that permanent habit harmed his performance, which just goes to show: be careful what you're practicing.

Practice Is Key to Performance

Teams train all week following their manager's plan in order to perform for one ninety-minute match. But what do you do when the plan goes out the window? What do you do when the other team scores in the first five minutes, changing the whole dynamic of the game? What happens when you go a man down in the thirty-fifth minute?

At that point, you have to rely on the skills you have at hand, the skills you've practiced over time to deal with the big setbacks. Those skills you practiced hour after hour become the permanent instincts that allow for high-quality performance in challenging times. It's those instincts that allow players to find one another on the pitch without a glance. Those same instincts tell them when to jump into a tackle and when not to. In a game, we don't rise to the level of our opponents; we drop to the level of our training.

To perform with that level of instinct, though, you need to have practiced the right skills so you can pull them out when the time comes.

(Focus + Discipline) x Repetition = Excellence

The body and brain have an incredible ability to remember those things we repeat—both the good actions and the bad. Perform an action often enough, and it creates a neural pathway your brain follows every time you are in a particular situation. That's why we can clean our teeth without thinking about it. It's why we can follow the same workout routine every time we enter the gym. Those actions become habits. They're automated, as we covered in chapter 6.

In that chapter, we were focusing on the side of automation that frees up your time and energy. Now, we need to consider it from a performance perspective. Essentially, are you creating the habits that help you perform and overcome setbacks, or are you building habits that hold you back? Do you have any habits that act in your life the same way Seaman's habit of picking up back passes hurt his team's performance?

If you do, now is the time to eliminate them and start practicing the kind of habits you want to see become permanent. That's one of the most significant keys to consistently performing at a high level.

Practice the Right Things

In Seaman's case, it wasn't really his fault that he kept making those errors. He practiced according to the rules at the time. He couldn't have anticipated that those rules would change. Most of the time, though, we know which habits would help us perform and which wouldn't. All we have to do is practice the right things.

If you create a habit of checking your phone every five minutes, that is going to hurt your efficiency. It's going to slow down how quickly you can get tasks done and how well you can focus on whatever task is at hand. The good news is, practicing the opposite can rewrite that habit. The same way Seaman eventually changed his instincts to pick up the ball on a back pass, you can rewrite a habit to constantly check your phone.

This also holds true of the habit you may have created around showing up late or coming to meetings unprepared. It's the same for habits around your health. You gain focus by training focus, improve in conversation by practicing conversation. You become a better listener if you practice listening.

During a training session when a player shows up mentally and focuses for the entire session, they increase their ability to stay focused during the game, even when the pressure is on.

If you want better habits, you have to start by practicing better behaviors. So, what are you practicing every day? Are you getting up on time or hitting snooze three times before opening your eyes? Are you following your schedule or skipping tasks? Are you getting to work on time or showing up ten minutes late? Are you prepping for meetings, responding on time, focusing on each conversation, and taking the stairs rather than the elevator?

The more you make the right choices, the easier those choices become—until they become natural. They become as automatic as your first touch.

Practice Discipline

The brain is like a muscle; the more we practice something the correct way, the stronger it gets. The more we push hard in the areas that matter, the more those tasks become easier and reflexive. And this is particularly valuable when we practice discipline.

If you push through and do that final set on leg day, the next week it's a little easier to complete that set. Give it a few more weeks, and you won't even think of skipping it. In fact, you'll be ready for a new, harder challenge.

And this isn't just true within the sphere you're currently focusing your efforts. The more you show that discipline in your workouts, the easier it is to be disciplined in other areas. If you can push yourself for that last set, you can also push yourself to finish your paperwork on time. You can push yourself to cook a healthy dinner instead of eating out. Discipline fosters more discipline.

The author and ex–Navy Seal Jocko Willink has a fantastic phrase that he uses: disciple equals freedom. It's the perfect dichotomy to describe everything in work and life. If you have the *discipline* to work hard when you *don't need to*, then you will have the *freedom* to *not* work hard when *you have to*. If you want more financial freedom, then practice discipline in your spending when you don't have to. If you want more freedom with your time, then practice discipline in your work to reduce how long you have to spend in the office. If you want the freedom to enjoy the weekend with the family, then practice discipline and work out every weekday so you have the energy to go on those big family adventures. And so on.

We become disciplined by practicing discipline. And that discipline opens up a world of possibilities.

Showing Up

Another key area where we can use "practice to make permanent" to particular effect is showing up. Showing up is not just about the physical act of being in the right place on time; it's just as much about being psychologically present and ready to perform.

Far too often, people reduce showing up to just getting to the right location. As long as you turn up to training or at the office, this thinking goes, then that is half the battle. As long as you put the hours in, you can pat yourself on the back. The rest will take care of itself. This is why most people actually only work twenty hours each week; they just take forty hours to do it.

But this is all wrong. When you show up for practice, you have to practice being ready to not only be there on the field physically but mentally. You have to cross the white line—and not just do it for those ninety-minute sessions at certain points during the day. Then, just like those muscles you strengthen through an extra set, showing up will become easier and more natural—something you do every time you have to and that you can do for extended periods.

You practice it, and it becomes permanent.

Choose Your Habits

Showing up is just one more example where a permanent new habit can lead to permanent new highs in your performance. It certainly isn't the only one.

The main lesson here is that whatever quality you need that will bring you up to the next level at work or life, that's the one you should practice. Teams that struggle with passing spend more time passing in training. When a team isn't scoring enough goals, what do you think they focus on every day of the week? Finishing.

The same should be true in your own life. Practice those qualities that will make the most difference and do it every day. At the same time, be relentless with *how* you practice it. Have a clear plan and execute that plan. Review your progress and then get back to practice. Whether you are a CEO, coach, teacher, or stay-at-home parent—practice may not make you perfect, but it can permanently improve your performance.

Game Time

What are your top three areas of improvement or your biggest three weaknesses?

1.

2.

3.

What are the next actionable steps you can "practice" or implement to improve them? What do you need to do to make your weaknesses your strengths?

For example, if you feel you're always checking your phone, you could put it on silent at select times during the day. You could turn off social media notifications. Or you could set screen-free times each day.

All of these would improve your focus and performance while reducing your attention wasted on your phone.

CHAPTER 9

Daily Improvement

Early on in Frank Lampard's career, there were some question marks over his potential. When he came into the West Ham first team, his uncle, Harry Redknapp, was the manager of the club. His father was the assistant coach. Some fans wondered if the future "Super Frank" was getting special treatment.

Redknapp was asked about this at a fan forum. He was unequivocal. Not only was Frank good enough for West Ham, "He will go right to the very top—right to the very top."[4]

In 2022, when the team at FootballJOE showed Redknapp that clip, the former manager explained his reasoning.

"He had such a fantastic attitude," Redknapp recalled. "I'd look out of my office, and it would be four o'clock, and he'd be out on the pitch still … raining, snowing, whatever. He'd be out there doing sprints, shooting, getting a bag of balls on his own, hitting shots, collecting balls. I knew with that attitude … I knew he was going to go do what he did."

---

4   FootballJOE, "Right to the Very Top," July 18, 2022, 1:19 p.m., https://x.com/FootballJOE/status/1549081437755826177.

The skeptical fans had been wrong. Lampard had a world of talent that led to one of the greatest midfield careers in Premier League history. But Redknapp knew the deeper reason his nephew would be a success: every day, he was doing what he had to do to be a little better than the day before.

Do that long enough, and the exceptional truly becomes possible.

Relentless Commitment

High achievers all have one thing in common: a growth mindset. They back themselves to improve. They believe that hard work and consistent effort lead to relentless, incremental improvement. And that is a formula that can yield enormous results.

0.1% Improvement x Time = Exponential Gains

This mindset can make a huge difference. And the numbers add up more quickly than you might think. If you made just a 0.1 percent improvement each day in any area of your life, that would give you an annual gain of almost 50 percent in that area.

This is the essence of the marginal gains theory, the idea of constant improvement for radical new results. That idea led to Team GB dominating the cycling world under Sir David Brailsford. It also turned Lampard into a champion. To this day, Lampard is the only midfielder to appear on the top twenty all-time Premier League goal scorers list. And he comes in at number six! That is astounding for a midfielder. Think of all the great strikers in the Premier League who have scored fewer goals than Frank Lampard, all because he combined his talent with that little extra effort each day.

Marginal improvement takes less effort than you might assume. You don't have to start out staying late and training in the rain like Lampard to start seeing benefits. If you're reading twenty pages a day right now, ask yourself a very simple question: Can you read one more sentence each day than you read the day before?

One-tenth of 1 percent of twenty pages of text works out to about six words. That's not much, right? It might take you a couple seconds. But if you kept adding six more words to your reading time every day for a year, you'd end up reading several more books than you otherwise would have.

And how many more words would you need to read on the 365th day of your incremental process? It wouldn't be pages and pages of text. It would be just six more words than the day before.

This example highlights the part of this process that is actually the most difficult. It isn't the 0.1 percent improvement that is hard to manage; it's the consistent, daily effort to add that 0.1 percent on top of what you're already doing.

To do anything at the highest level requires a relentless commitment to doing it a little better every single day. If you can manage that, you gain a new ally in your efforts: the law of compound interest. That law states that small deposits with even modest rates of improvement lead to huge gains. That's true of your retirement account, but it's equally true of anything you choose to put focus on—so long as you truly commit.

Can I Perform Better than Yesterday?

Anthony Gordon's favorite book is *Winning* by Tim Grover. In it, Grover describes what separates those who go on to do remarkable things from those who fall short. As a private coach for Michael Jordan and Kobe Bryant, he'd certainly know the difference. And part of the formula for that level of success, he says, comes down to how you understand a concept like winning. Ask a random person what the word winning means to them, and they'll throw out positive, joyful words: euphoric, amazing, incredible. But when Grover asked his top clients what the word brought to their minds, the answers were starkly different: horrible, lonely, dark.

It wasn't that these winners were all depressed. They simply knew the hard road—the grind—required to reach the top. They weren't experiencing winning as a metaphor or a dream. They lived it as a reality.

Progress—even incremental progress—is supposed to hurt. It's supposed to be uncomfortable. That little voice inside your head encouraging you to stop, that is growth in disguise. Just beneath that voice is another, a quieter voice with greater conviction. It's a voice asking how you can perform better today than you did yesterday.

That first voice is very persuasive. Most people prefer to remain in their comfort zone. They are not willing to listen to the second voice that demands they put long-term gain ahead of short-term pain.

We may know that doing one more set before we head to the office prepares us for an entire day of clear thinking and focus, just like we know that saying no to those chips is better for our weight and overall health. We know that staying that extra few minutes in the office when everyone else has bailed for happy hour could land us a sale that eventually leads to our promotion, just like we know that it's better to go to bed than continue to binge *The Office* for the twelfth time. Yet it's all so tempting. Short-term gain is right now, and long-term pain seems so far away.

Minor Tweaks + Persistence = Major Improvements

This is why Lampard's behavior struck Redknapp as so extraordinary. Putting in the effort, doing that little bit more each day—even in a team of professionals, it was rare to see.

But how do you do it? If you are ready to listen to that second voice and do that little bit more each day, what exactly can you do to ensure you are always putting in a little more? It's one thing to talk about reading or gym exercises, but what about management, software development, or entrepreneurship? How do you put a little more effort in each day when you work in HR or as a stay-at-home parent?

There are two main areas you can concentrate on: subtracting what is slowing you down and adding more to what you do best.

ELIMINATE INEFFICIENCIES

This is the concept of addition by subtraction. While doing better today than yesterday feels like it has to be about adding—adding weight before a set, adding time to our workday—we can also see those modest improvements by slowly subtracting those things that are less helpful from our lives.

We already covered some of these activities when discussing bundling in chapter 4. Things like email, texting, and social media can suck up a lot of time for limited (or in some cases no) value. Subtracting this from our lives (either by bundling or simply choosing not to indulge at all) can save time and energy. It's eliminating waste.

But this isn't just about subtraction through bundling activities. We can look for areas to subtract everywhere. Consider the potential value from a hybrid schedule. You could save hours a week by cutting down the number of days you commute. By regularly scheduling more work from home, you can increasingly save time each week.

You can also subtract your difficult customers. Most businesses spend the majority of their time on customers who bring in the least value. They're chronic complainers who demand special treatment. These customers are often the first to run to a competitor.

Of course, you probably can't part from all of them at once. So make incremental progress, choosing those you can most easily cut ties with and make further cuts when you can—until eventually your company is largely free of these problem customers.

By subtracting those customers from your business, you can spend more time with your top customers and prospects, increasing their investment in your company. Now that's a way to build on your strengths.

MULTIPLY STRENGTHS

As you subtract what is holding you back, take all those gains in time, focus, and energy and invest them in the incremental improvement of your strengths. If you're a great salesperson, don't take that for granted. There's always something you can learn—some skill you can further develop. The greatest successes in every field are autodidacts. They keep learning and developing even when they're at the top.

One of the best ways you can do this is simply by continuing to do what you're doing right this minute: reading (or, for some of you, listening). Successful people leave clues in the form of a book. Read the books of those who have succeeded in your field. Read the books of those who have succeeded in related fields—as well as completely different fields.

Then use what you learn to build on your strengths.

And make sure you're focused on strengths. There's a whole world of advice that recommends we strengthen at our weakest points. It's true that there's some value in improving in a weak area if it's critical to your success or if you are particularly bad at it, but the majority of your energy should go into those skills where you're strongest.

Do you think Beckham spent much time practicing with his left foot? Rivaldo hardly ever kicked a ball with his right foot in his life—because he didn't need to.

If you're great at math and struggle with languages, build on those math skills. Leave the language needs within your business to those who are naturally adept at it. Then, once you know where you want to strengthen, put that incremental improvement philosophy into practice. Read a little more, practice a little more each day—and watch as the benefits come.

Making the Tough Choice

Investing is hard work. We'd all rather spend our entire paycheck and enjoy ourselves than save for retirement and our kids' college. We have to miss out on a lot of fun to build our financial future.

The same is true of every part of our lives. It would absolutely be more fun to eat pizza and drink beer every day, skip every workout, and sleep in every morning. But just as incremental daily improvement can lead to spectacular success, so can incremental poor decision-making lead to worse and worse outcomes. The world of soccer is littered with careers of players who did the opposite of Frank Lampard, putting in a little less effort each day.

If we want to truly perform in any field, we have to make the tough choices every single day. And that requires a high level of mental toughness, which is where we're heading next.

Game Time

What's the smallest improvement you can make today? And I mean the *smallest*. When you think of an example, push yourself to come up with an even smaller step.

Once you have something truly miniscule in mind, commit to it. And build on it every day from there.

CHAPTER 10

Mental Toughness

In February 2011, Arsenal was in dangerous form. They'd won four of their last five, drawing that fifth match against Manchester City. Only Everton had managed to score a goal against them in the new year. Their run of form saw them closing the gap on league leaders Manchester United. In the air was the hope that Arsène Wenger could lead the Gunners to their first title in almost a decade.

You could have forgiven the players of Newcastle United for feeling overwhelmed by the prospect of hosting one of the top sides in the league. After all, the Magpies were having an indifferent season, bobbing around in midtable.

If Newcastle was having nightmares before the match, nothing could have prepared them for what the first half actually looked like when goal after Gunner goal rained in. Theo Walcott started things off by scoring for Arsenal in the first minute. That's right, minute one, Arsenal was ahead. It only got worse from there. In the third minute, Andrey Arshavin swung a free kick into the box for Johan Djourou to knock into the back of the net.

Arsenal just kept coming. In the tenth minute, Walcott sent a ball into the six-yard box and found a completely unmarked Robin van Persie, a man who didn't miss from that close. 3-0. To finish Newcastle off, Bacary Sagna sent another ball flying into the area where van Persie was yet again unmarked. After twenty-six minutes, the game was as dead as they come. Newcastle was down by four. Their only hope was to try to close up shop and hope they could prevent Arsenal racking up a cricket score.

At that point, you could hardly blame a few of the Newcastle faithful for leaving, throwing their tickets down in disgust.

But the game wasn't over. In the second half, Newcastle showed incredible fight. Joey Barton came in for a tough tackle, and Arsenal's Abou Diaby recklessly reacted, pushing Barton and gearing up for a fight. He was sent off in the fiftieth minute. That was the bit of good luck the team from Tyneside needed. In the sixty-eighth minute, Leon Best earned a penalty. Barton took it and took it well. Newcastle had one back.

The Magpies had so much belief, they harried the Arsenal keeper to get the ball back so they could restart play. Seven minutes later, that belief paid off again, as Best knocked the ball down with his first touch and then snuck one past the keeper to close the gap to two goals. With the crowd going mental, Newcastle earned another penalty with seven minutes to go, which Barton diligently scored.

From an easy romp, Arsenal was desperately clinging on. When Newcastle won a free kick in the eighty-seventh minute, every Gunner was in the box to defend it. They cleared Barton's kick but only as far as Cheick Tioté, who sent it screaming in from twenty-five yards out. From 4-0 down, they'd drawn Arsenal 4-4 in one of the greatest comebacks in Premier League history.

Embrace the Struggle

Desire + Work Rate = Success

No matter how well we plan, we will come up against difficulties. Sometimes, even with the best plan, you'll find yourself down 1-0 before you can blink. Sometimes, you'll be down 2-0 before you can catch your breath. Instead of fearing these moments, though, we should embrace them.

There is little satisfaction in beating an easy team, and there's little pride in success when the road was straight and level. On the other hand, there is no greater feeling than doing what Newcastle did: taking the field against stronger, bigger, faster opposition, and against all odds, coming out victorious—and yes, I'm classifying a 4-4 draw as a victory in this case.

Embracing that struggle not only prepares us for the inevitable moments of difficulty ahead, but it also creates room for more growth. We cannot grow by staying within our comfort zone. We have to challenge ourselves and be challenged by external events.

A good player does not advance themselves in their craft by playing against poor teams. They learn by challenging themselves to defeat the best in their league. There's a reason great players are so desperate to play for teams competing in the Champions League. It isn't just the chance to win glory and raise the trophy at the end of the season—it's the chance to test themselves against the best of the best in the world.

They know it will raise their game. They know it will make them dig deep and pull out a performance. Do that enough times, and those great sides go from an anomaly to their new benchmark. It is no longer the great opposition they once feared. It's the standard—and that means the level of their performance has also hit a new standard.

You'll have to hit these new standards if you truly want to achieve your dreams. Think about your own goals. Whether you want to become CEO one day, make your own company the biggest in your industry, or simply save enough to someday move to Southern California so you can go surfing every morning, at some point, you're going to be Newcastle facing an Arsenal. You are going to go up against a bigger competitor with more resources at their disposal. Don't fear it. Don't try to avoid it. Embrace it. Learn to love the challenge. This is the chance to test your mettle, to see where you fall short, and to find new resources within yourself.

Being 4-0 down in twenty-six minutes is no one's idea of a great start to a match, but those Newcastle players discovered they had more courage and motivation than they might have ever imagined by finding it within themselves to keep going and driving for that draw. Coming back from being 4-0 down to draw at 4-4 is an exponentially better feeling than an easy 3-0 win. Don't deny yourself that same opportunity.

Don't Blame Circumstances

One of the best ways to rise to the level of your challenges is to refuse to give yourself the excuse of blaming your circumstances. We've all seen this. A team goes out and plays a tough game but comes away unlucky. Instead of looking inward, the players or the coach immediately point to the referee. The ref missed a penalty call. The linesman should have flagged offside. That second yellow was uncalled for.

These can often be accurate statements, but they don't help anyone grow or improve from these situations. After all, complaining about the refereeing is more likely to lead to a fine than to change a decision. If you lost on that account, don't complain. Accept it. Learn from it. Work harder for the next one. The aim should be to make sure that next time your team wins, no matter how bad the refereeing is.

This also holds true for our mindset before games. It's easy to start making excuses before we have to perform. We're still nursing that injury or there are too many games coming too quickly against top competition. We excuse a loss before we even lose.

We have to be braver, accept those tough circumstances, perform as well as we can, and then learn everything possible from the results.

Dig Deep

Much of this book is full of concrete tools to help you reach success, whether in planning, performing, or recovering/reviewing progress. But this lesson is more fundamental. It's about finding something deep within yourself that screams out "never" when you're up against it. Winston Churchill put it best: "Never give in—never, never, never, never, in nothing great or small, large or petty, never give in except to convictions of honor and good sense. Never yield to force; never yield to the apparently overwhelming might of the enemy."

There comes a time in the tough games when you have to grind out a result with a few minutes left. Your legs are tired, your mind is exhausted, you can hardly catch your breath. Somehow, you have to find it within yourself to pull out the best part of your performance for the entire match. It may only be five minutes, but those five minutes feel like an eternity.

Everything hurts. Your lungs are burning. Every part of your body and mind is telling you that there's no way you can keep this intensity up for another moment, let alone another five minutes.

And yet, champions are able to find that extra gear in those tough moments. They're able to dig deeper than anyone else. That's what allowed Newcastle to get a draw against Arsenal. It's what allowed Manchester United to come back and complete the treble in the 1999 Champions League final.

Like Newcastle in 2011, in life and business, we should aim to never give in. Sure, there are times when reality is too much to surmount. In business in particular, we can look around at some shocking failures and think those leaders definitely should have given up a lot sooner before they burned through all that cash. But we can't let those examples become our dominant narrative—we can't let them become our excuse. Because we also have some breathtaking examples of business leaders who showed such unbelievable grit and determination that they beat even the toughest odds and changed the world. Everything hurt, everything was going wrong, but they held on until they had the victory.

Consider Elon Musk. I know he's become more controversial of late, but there's a lot we can learn from him and his career. He had a great start to his entrepreneurial career. He made $20 million on his first business, and then $180 million on PayPal. Brilliant, right? He must have thought he could do no wrong.

His next moves were to invest in SpaceX and Tesla. Both of these companies were cash burners. Imagine a product that costs about $20 million to launch where a small coding mistake can lead to that entire product exploding. There's not much you can save from a rocket that blows up and then burns up on reentry. Around 2008, when the financial crisis hit and banks had stopped lending, Elon had said he had enough money for three attempts to get a rocket into orbit. All three exploded.

Meanwhile, the Tesla Roadster ended up becoming an expensive debacle. It took years before Tesla was even able to make a profit on each car they sold. To keep their doors open, Tesla had to do a round of layoffs because the company had run out of cash.

In that circumstance, many people would give up. They'd salvage what they could of their investment and put their money in something safer. What did Musk do? He dug in. He had so much belief in himself and his companies that he handed over his last $20 million from the PayPal sale. Imagine that. He put up the last of the $180 million he had made, an amount that would have set him up for a life of complete luxury.

And it paid off. The fourth rocket was a success, earning SpaceX a $1.2 billion NASA contract. Daimler would then invest in Tesla, saving that company as well. From four down, Musk came back to win the match.

In my own way, I've experienced a similar difficult path to success. To get my company off the ground, I had to buy a commercial building for an indoor soccer complex. Unfortunately, I decided to follow this dream in 2009, at the height of the Great Recession when nobody was lending money. I went to thirty banks, all of which said no. Then, the thirty-first bank said "maybe," which eventually turned into a "yes."

At the time, my wife and I had just bought our first house and had newborn twins. Suddenly, I was borrowing millions of dollars to build the facility and pledging everything to the bank as collateral. It was a very risky choice, but I didn't focus on that. I was determined to dig in and make sure it worked out.

If we want to achieve anything big in our lives—whether it's on the pitch, in entrepreneurship, in sales at a large corporation, or in our own families—we're going to have to take big chances, believe in ourselves, and dig deep when things aren't going our way. It might be taking out a big loan to open your restaurant, chasing that big client when everyone says it's a fool's errand, or putting in the hours at night to retrain in a new area despite the tough odds of turning it into a career. Whatever it is, you have to dig deep. You know what the right thing to do is.

When you dig deep and make those positive actions, you become a player everyone fears. You'll be the player who has that little something extra—one of the players the competition knows will never give up, a player who performs the miracles that show up in the big games and win leagues.

Never Give Up

"Never give up" is something we're taught from the earliest age, and yet, so many of us fail to absorb it. There have been so many examples of great comebacks in soccer, but we tend to remember the games like Newcastle versus Arsenal because they are actually pretty rare. Victories that make the hairs on the back of your neck stand up, time stand still, and your heart race out of control never leave you. Despite our love of these victories, though, it's far more common to see teams give up, to see them try to limit the severity of a loss or just to hang their heads and jog around the pitch, just waiting for the game to end. When you're in the midst of a game like that, the unlikely victory seems so far away that it can feel impossible.

When we perform, we have to remember this is a false impression: the impossible is often possible—and the only way to know for sure is to keep fighting.

Unlike soccer players, we aren't just performing for ninety minutes. We need that fighting attitude to stay with us across all the hours, days, weeks, months, and years ahead to hit our goals. Perseverance and persistence are two of the most important characteristics in business, and we have to bring them to every effort we make to tackle the biggest obstacles in our life. No matter the odds, that persistence is what separates those who can say, "Look at what I have achieved" from those who lament, "Look at what I almost did."

No matter what the circumstances, there is always something you can do to influence the outcome in your favor, as long as you don't give up. I speak from experience. I compete in triathlons. At some point in every event, every athlete runs into what I call the "dark cave of pain." There are only two ways to get through it: either you give up or you push through the cave to the other side. If you give up, you can risk staying in that dark cave forever—because the regret of quitting may never leave you. Considering that, the best option is clear: you keep going.

It's the same when performing on your plans. At some point, it's going to feel like it's too much. Life is too busy. It's too tiring. The competition is too tough. It just feels so much simpler to start negotiating your nonnegotiables or to walk away entirely.

In those moments, instead of giving in, channel your inner Newcastle. When it gets tough, double down. If you push through the dark cave, you'll find that you are capable of performing at a higher level than you ever thought possible—and achieving more than you ever dreamed.

Game Time

Think back to a time when you gave up on something too soon. List what things you could have done to keep going, to stay in the game.

Use this as motivation for the next tough moment that presents itself. If failure was that bad before, isn't it worth pushing a little harder this time?

CHAPTER 11

Don't Jump into Every Tackle

There's a lot of passion in the game of soccer. It's part of what we love about the sport. But sometimes, those high emotions get the best of players to disastrous effect.

I'm sure you can think of your own favorite examples of this. I often think of David Beckham kicking out at Diego Simeone in the 1998 World Cup. Simeone had been pushing Beckham's buttons all match, and after one particularly rough shove in the back while contesting a header, Beckham let his emotions get the better of him. He petulantly flicked his heel up into Simeone's thigh. Watching the video now, many years divorced from the intensity of that match, it's easy to see Beckham barely glanced him. It probably wasn't worth the red card it earned—but it did earn a red card.

England went on to lose that match.

He wasn't the only hothead to ever play a World Cup match, of course. Another great example is Zinedine Zidane, who lost control during the 2006 World Cup final when he famously headbutted Marco Materazzi in the chest after some trash talk he took particular offense to. The result was the same: a red card and game over for France.

It isn't just the players who lose their head sometimes. It can be a whole club. After James Rodriguez won the Golden Boot in the 2014 World Cup, Real Madrid went in for him for an eye-watering $86 million. The results were … fine. He had a decent first season before becoming a bench player and quietly moving on for free a few years later. That was clearly not the career Madrid expected after their impulse purchase.

The lessons here are clear. If you want to win, it isn't just about pushing through the hard moments in your performance or having the discipline to make incremental improvements. There's also immense value in keeping your head every time you have to perform.

The Power of Saying No

Perhaps the most common example of hotheaded decision-making in the game is the rash tackle. A player jumps into a tackle two-footed, moving too quickly, and risks a red card or an injury when a more subtle defense would have been more effective. It's a symptom of letting the emotion of the moment make the decision instead of your best judgment. It's a sign of lost focus.

To avoid those tackles takes a certain maturity, an ability to step back from the moment and realize if it really helps the team to dive in like that. Sometimes, the answer is still yes, but most of the time, it's better to remain focused on your ultimate goals and avoid overcommitting.

Staying focused doesn't just mean concentrating on the item at hand. It also means saying "no" to everything else. To avoid jumping into every tackle, you have to be deliberate and ask the question, "Will saying yes to this move me toward my actual goals?"

Steve Jobs has a great quote on this exact point:

"People think focus means saying yes to the thing you've got to focus on. But that's not what it means at all. It means saying no to the hundred other good ideas that there are. You have to pick carefully. I'm actually as proud of the things we haven't done as the things I have done. Innovation is saying no to thousands of things."

The most successful businesspeople have all developed the fine art of saying no. They realize that by saying yes to a request, they are effectively saying no to something else that is already on their to-do list. We do the same in family life. Commitment to anyone, after all, is an agreement to say no to everyone else.

At this point, you have a solid list of tasks that you know will lead to your goals. You have planned time to get to those priorities. If you're going to allow something else to wrestle into your day and draw your attention away in performance, it really needs to be worth your while. This tackle has to be crucial for you to jump in. In other words, you only jump in if it's a ball worth winning.

Changing this mindset makes it a lot easier to say no to opportunities, requests, and invitations. It makes it easier to cut those unnecessary tasks that we continue to cling to. Even when we emotionally feel compelled to commit to something, we have to be willing to step back and think clearly about our current responsibilities and whether it's worth jumping into this one two-footed.

This ability to turn down opportunities is valuable not just because it helps us remain focused, but because it also helps us perform against others. Remember, we aren't competing in a vacuum. When we dive into tackles, we risk more than just a red card if we get our timing wrong. Seasoned competitors may simply skip past us. Steve Jobs, Bill Gates, and Sir Alex Ferguson all had the same amount of time in a day as any of us. They all had children, family responsibilities, and social pastimes. They all had younger, more energetic, and enthusiastic competitors to deal with on an ongoing basis. But they stayed razor focused and said no to every opportunity that wasn't right at that moment. If they'd done otherwise, I might be writing about those young, enthusiastic competitors instead, because just a little distraction might have been enough to allow those competitors to skip past them and go on to score those big goals.

Focus on What You Control

This isn't an easy skill to master. In the moment, when we're pumped up and ready to compete, it's easy to get overwhelmed and make a rash decision. To avoid that, we have to pull back into ourselves and focus on our own game. In other words, don't worry about the other team; play your game.

This isn't to say that a team should avoid preparing for the opposition. We all know that every team studies the players and strategy of their opponents before the match. They predict tactics and try to counter them. They aim to neutralize the opposition's most dangerous players and set up in a way that gives them the best chance of winning.

But once the planning is done, the performance is often mostly about how we perform. If your left back puts in the performance of his life and tracks every run the other team's star right winger makes, that may be the defining aspect of the game. Tracking back and defending well are within that player's control. In that sense, it isn't about what tricks the right winger is planning to throw at the defender. If the defender plays his game right, that right winger is probably not getting through.

There may be something that that right winger can do that the left back can't defend against, but it isn't really worth worrying about that or wasting time thinking about it. Instead, that left back has to focus on everything they do and making sure they commit to their role fully.

This isn't new advice. You'll find it in the famous Serenity Prayer that every addict learns: "God, grant me the serenity to accept the things I cannot change, the courage to change the things I can, and the wisdom to know the difference."

In other words, give me the wisdom to know when to jump into a tackle and when to stay on my feet. Give me the courage to go in full force when I have to make that tackle and give me the composure to accept that there are things the other player can do that I can't control.

This lesson is so universal because it isn't really about soccer or addiction. It's about everything. In a sale, there are certain parts of the process you have control over—the quality of your pitch, the frequency and quality of your communication client, the clothes you wear, the tone of your voice, your punctuality—and there are things beyond your control. Ultimately, there's nothing you can do to dissuade a client from choosing your competitor.

The same is true if you have a boss who's a Muppet. Don't worry about it. Keep your head down and work hard. That boss will most likely get found out soon enough by someone who has control over their employment destiny.

Or maybe they won't. But no matter what happens to them, you control the quality of your work and whether you keep working there.

That's one of the most crucial lessons in defending in soccer. Watch any great defender, and they don't get flustered by all the fancy stepovers, turns, and pullbacks. They don't dive into those tackles because they aren't fooled by the feet of the forward dribbling at them. Their eyes are locked on the ball. They know what matters, and they stay focused on it.

No matter how intense the occasion or how great the player they're facing, they know that all they control is their position and their movement, and the only thing that matters is that the ball at the forward's feet doesn't make it anywhere near their keeper's net.

Always Put on a Performance

No matter what our goals or what our career and lives look like, we are certain to face tough opposition. There will be times when we are that left back facing down Mbappé. And there are times when Mbappé will skip past us and score a worldie.

There are also going to be games when we just aren't up for it—when everything seems to go wrong. Our touch abandons us, every pass is misplaced, we slip on the grass and allow an easy chance. There will be times when we're cold and nursing an injury and just trying to make it to full time.

It's unavoidable. It's life. But that doesn't mean we give up and just accept a poor performance. The quality of your skill on the day isn't always within your control, but the effort is. That's why I always tell my team that there's no excuse for ever giving below a seven-out-of-ten performance.

Every player has games when they're just not at it. But they can always avoid a low rating by doing the fundamental things right. Nothing stops you from running to close down an opponent and running to create some space for your team. You may not be making great passes, but you can leave yourself open to receive the ball. You can get dirty and make the hard tackles.

The same is true in your life. You'll have days when you aren't as eloquent in front of investors and your judgment is off when fine-tuning a new product. You'll have days when you don't feel like mom or dad of the year. But you can still show up, check off tasks, put the effort in, and earn a seven out of ten. You can do it at home, doing the chores, putting the kids to bed, and at least cooking some instant mac and cheese instead of ordering out.

That's not the level of performance you want every day, but sometimes, when you can't do anything else, it's good enough.

Game Time

List five things that are in your control in your life and five things that are not.

PART III

Recover

CHAPTER 12

Postgame Review

Every successful team does the same thing after a game. Win, lose, or draw, the team will come in the day after and do a "warm down" to recover from fatigue. This involves, among other things, some light exercise to help the muscles recover after a tough performance. The point is to give their bodies some much needed rest. They'll also review the game they played the day before. They'll look at tape of the game and discuss what went well, what went wrong, and what they could do better.

They'll use this information to plan for the week ahead. They'll highlight areas they need to practice in training. If the team let the opposition score a set piece goal, they'll spend time training on defense of set piece plays for that week. If the team struggled to hold possession in transition, they'll concentrate on that on the training pitch.

All of this comes together so the team can perform better in the next match. In other words, improved performance requires everyone to recover from a tough game and to review how the performance went. That's the only way to improve.

Review Everything

Just like the professional soccer teams we admire, we all have to take the time to recover and review our plans, performance, and progress. In the next chapter, we'll discuss taking actual time off to truly rest. Here, we'll focus on those "warm down" days in which our work is focused solely on review. Depending on the length of time you're reviewing (from a day to a year), this will require more or less "warm down" time. Like the players, this is work in a sense, but it's less intense than what we do during peak performance. Essentially, this is a version of the breaks we take between those ninety-minute sessions we plan.

When we're in warm-down mode, we should be open to reviewing everything. Like a good manager, everything has to be on the table: what we're doing well, what we're doing poorly, and whether we're doing the right things at all. For that reason, you'll want to take these periods to review your goals over the short and long term. You'll want to review your Big Three. Have you concluded one of them? Is some new task suddenly much more impactful?

You can review what you've been batching. Are all of your batches working? Could you batch other tasks together? Are certain batched items reducing your ability to complete those tasks effectively?

Also like players, you'll want to create a dedicated time and place for these warm-down reviews. Players go to the training ground after a game specifically for these review sessions. You can do yours in your office, in a café, or in your car—they can be done before work, over lunch, or during a slow hour on Friday—but make sure there's a place and time you know you'll get to this. The key is, whatever you choose, you do this at the same time and the same place each week.

Additionally, as you review, take notes on your findings. Don't just trust yourself to remember everything. Instead, you should log everything. Whether it's in a journal, in your notes app on your phone, or in a recorded message you send yourself, make sure all your findings are stored somewhere so you can build those discoveries into your plans moving forward. There's real value in doing this with the pen and paper method, but if keeping this digital is more likely to get you to stick with it, then go with that.

Finally, as you go through all these reviews, focus on remaining positive. It's important to consider your shortfalls, but it does you no good to beat yourself up too much. I recommend trying to balance praise and criticism of yourself in all your reviews to hit an eighty-twenty split. Eighty percent of your notes should be positive, focusing on what you're doing right. The remaining 20 percent can hit what you didn't achieve. But even here, focus on how you can improve in those areas going forward. For example, instead of writing "I missed three workouts this week," write "I won't miss any workouts next week."

Daily Review

Because this process is cyclical, we touched on all of the following reviews at the beginning of this process, back in chapter 2. Here, though, I want to dig into each review on a deeper level, so you have all the knowledge you need to start reviewing performance across all timelines.

The daily review is a very short activity. You can probably complete this in five minutes at the end of the workday or at some point in your evening. Regardless, do this before you go to bed. The Zeigarnik Effect—named for Lithuanian psychologist Bluma Zeigarnik—proves that when you plan your day the night before, your brain will subconsciously start working to solve the problems overnight.

The review process begins with simply checking off all the tasks completed over the course of your day. Then you can tally up your successes and give yourself a score. If you have seven tasks on your list and complete five, you get a five out of seven for the day.

You should also track the time spent on your Big Three. Each one of your Big Three should get about an hour of your time each day. This, of course, fluctuates depending on what those Big Three tasks are, but as a general rule an hour per task should be the baseline. You can also give yourself a score for how many hours you spent on these (which you can then log on the scoreboards you set up in chapter 7).

Reviewing your scores, ask yourself whether this was a good day. Keep in mind that stuff happens to all of us that complicates our plans. For instance, a three out of seven for items on your list and one out of three hours spent on your Big Three might be a pretty unproductive and "bad" day when everything is otherwise organized and going according to plan. But some days you'll have an unexpected call from a client or an unplanned lunch with a friend who is only in town for a couple days. If you manage three out of seven and one out of three on those days, you've done well. In fact, it's probably been a great day!

And, of course, there will also be days when you simply couldn't get to those priority actions at all. That's okay. Focus on how you can get back on track the next day. Teams lose—and sometimes lose badly. Instead of focusing on the failure, look for ways to improve your planning and performance the next time you have to show up. After all, you can lose a few games and still have a great season.

Weekly Review

I usually do the weekly review on Friday afternoon between 1:00 and 2:00 p.m. because it's a nice warm-down activity before I head into the weekend. It also leaves me a little time to catch any tasks I missed for the week. But it's just as easy to perform this one over the weekend.

The main element of this review is what I call the "daily planner purge." Start by reviewing your notes and action items from your daily planner over the week. What tasks did you miss? Is there anything you really needed to do but kept putting off? In particular, pay attention to any potential Big Three items that you've missed for the week.

At the same time, look for other areas where tasks may have fallen through the cracks. Review your texts, voicemails, and emails. Did you promise to complete any items there? Is there anything you're promising to deliver next week? Almost 100 percent of the time, I catch something that I have missed during the week simply by reviewing these messages.

You can also take this time to collect and organize any "loose" items you've collected over the week. If you've got notes on scraps of paper, business cards from potential clients, notes in your notes app, or Post-its with reminders sitting around, now's your chance to organize them in your files and add any new items to your future lists.

Gather all the tasks you missed and all the new tasks you have to add to future plans and put these items down in your notes. Crucially, keep these notes *in a separate document or notebook* than your daily notes so that you can keep everything straight. This will allow you to review your weekly reviews more easily than if you have them mixed in with your daily notes.

Any new or missed tasks need to be added to next week's plan.

Finally, before you finish up, ask yourself a question: How do you feel about the week? Here, we're looking to be a little less scientific, focusing instead on a gut feeling. As you write out these general impressions, though, keep in mind that eighty-twenty positivity split. Even if things aren't going particularly well, focus more on what you're getting right and how you intend to improve.

Here's an example from my own notes, from November 2021:

"Great week. Early starts Monday to Friday. Got loads done, felt great, worked out well. The weather was nice and chilly as well. Got three evening reading sessions done."

And here's one from a less-than-ideal week at the end of January that same year:

"Another undisciplined week, although I did get in a swim, bike, and run. Tomorrow is February 1st. Time to draw a line in the sand. I need a solid month of ultra-discipline."

As you can see, these should be just short journal entries, but they can help you track your progress and motivate you whenever you reread them in later reviews.

Monthly Review

If you've done a good job with your weekly reviews, the monthly check-in doesn't take much time. Mostly, you're going to track how you've been working and what's changed in your plans. I'll provide a link to a full monthly review sheet in the Game Time section in this chapter. For now, though, here are some of the questions and prompts that I use to get a clear picture of my month:

- Identify new projects and create action lists.

- What tasks are taking 20 percent of my time and giving 80 percent of my results?

- What is giving me 20 percent of my results but taking 80 percent of my time?

- Who are the 20 percent of people who produce 80 percent of my enjoyment and propel me forward?

- Who are the 20 percent of people causing 80 percent of my setbacks and headaches?

- What is taking 80 percent of my energy for a 20 percent return?

- What are the top three activities that feel as though I have been productive?

- What's the one big thing I need to do next month to get me closer to my six-month goals?

- What goals next month will get me closer to my three-month goals?

There are also sections to fill out a someday/maybe list of goals that aren't in play at the moment, questions on habits and behavior patterns that are helping or hurting progress, and sections on the books you are reading, the things you are learning, and the times during the month when you were happiest.

All of this comes together to provide a clear portrait of where you have been for the month and where you are going.

Quarterly/Bi-Annual Review

These two reviews go together for two reasons. First, it really depends on the individual whether this is a quarterly or bi-annual activity. And second, the questions and process are the same either way.

The main aim in this review is to build on that monthly portrait to continue to see your progress across all the areas of your life while adding in any crucial new information that might change your medium- and longer-term goals. What has happened over the last quarter or six months? How has that affected you? How have you dealt with it?

The prompts in this review are as straightforward as they are in the monthly review—and like that review, a link to the form will be included at the end of the chapter.

Here are some of the central questions on that form:

- What have I struggled with over the last quarter/six months?

- What have I learned?

- What could I have done differently?

- What has really worked well for me?

There's also a section looking forward to the next quarter or six months. These questions include:

- What are my current goals? How do I intend to reach them?

- What are my set-in-stone plans over the next six months? How do I see these plans playing out? How do I want to feel when I accomplish those goals?

- What's missing in my life right now that I absolutely must include in the next six months?

- What would really light me up if I saw it happen?

You can fill out one of these reviews over a few hours either during your week or on the weekend. There are fewer questions here, and the aim is more aspirational. As you can probably tell, these questions aim to really drive up your motivation and find those areas that can make the biggest impact moving into the next quarter or six months.

Annual Review

Your annual review should come at the beginning of the new year. I tend to dedicate five days at the beginning of January to this. That might seem like a lot of time, but the benefits of this review are significant. They set up your entire year. This is essentially the work of a manager reviewing their entire season before preseason begins over the summer.

The reason this takes so long is that, like a thorough manager reviewing every game of the previous season, you go through all of your weekly, monthly, quarterly/bi-annual reviews and plans from the entire previous year. Part of the point is to take this process slowly. While taking five days of vacation for this is a valuable use of that time, you can also create this space in your work life simply using the lessons we've already covered in this book to free up more time. Go through everything week by week and month by month. Record all your thoughts on this review as you go, listing what went well and where you fell short.

What goals did you achieve? What goals did you miss? Why did you fall short of those goals? What stopped you from achieving them?

As we'll discuss in more detail in chapter 15, there should be some failures to review. A lack of any areas where you missed the mark is a failure in and of itself. It shows you haven't been ambitious enough.

With that in mind, you also want to look forward to the new year and consider what the best version of you looks like and where your ambitions are going to take you next. This is your time to reconsider your multiyear plan and whether you still want to hit those same targets. It's a time to reconsider your Big Three and plans you have for each quarter, month, week, and day.

The annual review has an annual version of the planner purge you'll be doing during the weekly review. It also includes a notepad purge, along with any other areas you store notes. From there, it asks you some key questions:

- What went well for the year? This is where you can list all your wins.

- What didn't go well? This is a space to consider where you fell short and why.

- What was I doing when I was achieving my best results?

- What mistakes did I make over and over?

- What did I learn?

The end of the review includes space for three lists:

- A list of what goes into your aspirational vision

- A list of your three-year goals

- A list of your annual goals

This is when you really set yourself up for the entire year, so don't skimp on time or focus. A manager who fails to review the previous season or plan for the next is likely to get sacked. Don't put yourself in that position.

Force Yourself to Make a Call

In chapter 12, I mentioned that I tell my team to always aim for seven-out-of-ten performances—because you can earn those on effort alone. However, sometimes, seven out of ten as a goal limits us. Whenever my managers have to give a score to the members of their teams, I set one restriction on their reviews: they can't give anyone on their team a seven out of ten. The reason for this is simple. It's the easiest score to give. So often, when you read reviews of soccer matches, the players all get seven out of tens, which translates to a performance in which they did fine. They didn't stand out. They didn't do too much wrong. They put the effort in, but they didn't wow anyone. It was just … fine. This is true in wins, loses, and draws.

Removing the "fine" option forces my managers to decide whether their people are doing well, with eight-out-of-ten performances, or poorly, with six-out-of-ten performances. In other words, it forces them to make a call and avoid the easy answers.

You can do the same with your own performance. While you can aim for seven out of ten on those tough days, when it comes to deciding how well you're doing overall, force yourself to commit. Instead of giving yourself a passing grade each week or each month or each year, make yourself be more brutally honest. Are you doing pretty well or pretty poorly? That answer is going to be far more useful in your review, your future plans, and your future performance.

You can still remain overall positive—a six-out-of-ten performance can improve to an eight out of ten next match if the player concentrates on the right things. But if you let that player keep sliding with seven out of tens, nothing is ever going to get better.

So force the issue, be honest, and use that honesty to improve. That's how you make a review really matter.

Game Time

Buy the notebooks necessary for your daily and weekly reviews. For the monthly and quarterly reviews, use the templates at www.soc-cerofsuccess.com. Then, all you have to do is block the time and start your review.

CHAPTER 13

The Formula for Growth

The year 2004 was a monumental year for Middlesbrough Football Club. It was the culmination of years of effort. The team had spent big on South American superstars. They had built a state-of-the-art training facility, the first of its kind in English soccer and a brand-new home, the Riverside Stadium, another first of its kind in design.

Boro also had a coaching staff that was emerging as one of the best in the country. Steve McClaren was manager. He had been an assistant manager at Manchester United during the famous treble season and would go on to manage the England national team. On staff he had a secret weapon: the quiet, unknown sports psychologist, Bill Beswick. At the time, a psychologist was unheard of in English soccer.

This was all the work of their chairman, Steve Gibson: a young local businessman who was Boro through and through. It was a tremendous accomplishment. But it had not brought the club any trophies. In fact, the club had failed to win any silverware since its formation in 1876.

And then, suddenly, it looked like Middlesbrough's luck was finally changing. Over two legs, Boro improbably defeated Arsène

Wenger's Arsenal to reach the League Cup final. The League Cup is one of only three top-tier domestic trophies in England, along with the Premier League and the FA Cup. It has been going since 1960. Now, Middlesbrough was one match from an incredible feat. After years of development and months of long, grueling battles across the season, they finally had their chance to win a trophy.

The final was on a Sunday, which made Friday a travel day down to London. The team's last training session before their date with destiny was Thursday. What did McClaren and Beswick plan for that final training session? Did they have some drills set up? Did they go for an intense workout? Did they spend hours watching tape of Bolton, their opposition?

Not at all. They arranged a tennis tournament. You read that right. Not tactics or speed work, patterns of play or set pieces, Boro was preparing for the final by playing tennis. Beswick believed that the players had been facing such physical and mental demands up to that point that they needed a complete break from the game. They needed to recover both mentally and physically so they could be at their very best on Sunday: hungry to play, hungry to win, and physically capable of the best performance of their lives.

Bill later reported at a lecture I attended that the players were laughing, competing, and cheating all afternoon. And no wonder, after months of stress and pressure, they finally had a chance to just enjoy themselves for a day.

With so much on the line, this might seem an odd way to prepare, but it paid off. Boro defeated Bolton 2-1. The trophy was lifted by their captain, Gareth Southgate, current England manager.

Why Rest Matters

In the last chapter, we focused more on the review component of this stage of the hat trick of success. While there is some recovery involved in taking the time to review your progress, I don't want to leave you with the impression that's the only rest you need. Sometimes, you just need to take a break.

Rest is important for all of us. Whether we like it or not, we need it. The word "burnout" has become very popular in our culture in recent years, and for good reason. Too many of us are trying to do too much without rest. At some point, the body and the mind just shut down. They demand time off. If you don't plan time for that rest and recovery, the mind and body can give out at the least convenient times.

This happens all the time over the course of a soccer season. Almost every season it seems some team overperforms in the league or in one cup competition or another. The pundits ask the same question each week: "Can they really do it?"

Then, somewhere around March or April, the results dip. Suddenly, the team can't buy a win. The reason is that the players have simply overexerted themselves for too long. They're burnt out.

This is one of the reasons the Premier League regularly debates whether it should take a break around Christmas. All the other top leagues in Europe—Spain's LaLiga, Germany's Bundesliga, Italy's Serie A, and France's Ligue 1—take a couple weeks off around the end of December for this exact reason.

Players are increasingly speaking out on this issue as well. In 2023, Real Madrid legend Raphaël Varane wrote on X about the risks to players' health that come from too many games and too little rest.

"From the managers and players," he shared. "We have shared our concerns for many years now that there are too many games, the schedule is overcrowded, and it's at a dangerous level for players physical and mental well-being."

If Varane needs a break, you can be sure that your mind and body do too. It's the only way to ensure you can continue to compete at your highest level.

Building Rest into Your Life

In the game of soccer there are several periods of rest built into how matches are played and when they're played. These periods of rest last for different amounts of time. Here's a quick breakdown:

- **A few minutes:** Several times within the game when players catch their breath, either because play slows down, there's an injury, or there's a natural pause in the play. These days, you'll also find these breaks during a VAR check.

- **Fifteen minutes:** Once a game, at halftime. Similar breaks are in place for extra time, when necessary.

- **Twelve to twenty hours:** Daily before and after games or between training sessions. The time includes sleep.

- **Two to three days off:** Once or twice per season, players are given these mini breaks to refresh.

- **Four weeks:** Annually, players usually get this time between the season ending and preseason starting.

If these breaks are required for the best players in the world to perform at the top level, why aren't we all doing the same thing? We think we can burn the midnight oil and get up early for another long day of work—and we think we can do it forever. The truth of the matter is, though, we are more productive with rest than without it.

Working fewer hours can be more productive than more hours with less rest.

Rest is a chance to reboot the brain and body—and it doesn't always require a week in the Caribbean to do that. Sometimes, all we need is a few minutes. If we schedule rest times into our lives, we become more productive and work when it's time to work.

We can do this using the same system for rest as soccer players:

- **A few minutes several times a day:** In our daily schedule, we have our ninety-minute blocks to do concentrated work as well as other periods of less focused work throughout the day. In between each of them, we should walk away from our desk and take a break.

- **Fifteen minutes:** This is our halftime in those ninety-minute blocks. It can also be used when we are "stuck" trying to fix a problem or complete a task. When we need to free up our mind to think more clearly, we can go for a walk, getting out of the work environment for a little while. We should also fit in at least fifteen minutes (and ideally thirty or more) to pull away from work and eat lunch without distractions.

- **Twelve to twenty hours:** This is the daily time you should take away from work.

- **Two to three days off:** These breaks represent long weekends you should add to your schedule for when you can truly unplug.

- **Four weeks:** Most of us aren't able to take four weeks off all at once the way soccer players are, but you should still aim for this amount of time away from your major responsibilities spread throughout the year.

To get the benefits of rest in these periods, you have to aim for true rest. If you commit to taking your mind and body completely away from your work environment for breaks that range from two minutes to four weeks, the results are staggering. But to do this, it requires commitment. When you're resting, don't look at your phone; don't answer an email. Let your brain rest. I know there are some of you who feel you can't take these breaks. Entrepreneurs believe they have to be on call 24-7. Parents feel they have to be involved in every moment of their children's lives. But unless your company is in crisis or you have a newborn, it's possible to get away at least some of the time. And you'll be better at what you do for taking that break.

Can I Be Better than Yesterday?

Stress + Rest = Growth

Rest is a key element of growth and success, but it isn't the only piece. When we return to work, we have to put ourselves in the stress of performance once again. That's the value of the rest. We rest so we can hit our top results when we're back on the pitch. Middlesbrough succeeded because the team rested and came back focused on performance and following through with their plans.

Progress is supposed to hurt. It's supposed to be uncomfortable. Uncomfortable times often turn out to be the most rewarding. As we've already covered, it's better to come back from 4-0 down than to cruise to a 3-0 victory if you want to really test yourself and improve. But that also means that we need breaks. When we come back refreshed, we can push ourselves to go a little harder, focus a little more intensely, and try the new things that could give us a real advantage.

So when you come back from a period of rest, you should ask yourself: How do I perform better? How can I perform better than last week? How can I come back and improve on my performance?

These are simple questions with huge consequences.

Most people fail to take breaks and so lack the energy to get out of their comfort zone. They are not able or willing to put long-term gain ahead of short-term pain. They're just too tired. They're exhausted, so they only do just enough. They stick with what they know. But what they know eats away at their time and energy, so they can't find new opportunities to get a break. The result of this cycle is burnout.

It's hard to get out of that rut. But if you add rest into your schedule where possible and focus on hitting new performance highs when you return, the space can open up for better results and more rest.

That's the best path toward sustained success.

Game Time

Schedule some time off to completely unplug and rest as soon as possible. Ideally, take one of those long weekends away. If you can't manage that, look for an opportunity to leave work early one day and focus on resting and rejuvenating that evening.

If you can't manage that, then commit to not checking email on your next weekend or two-day break.

Once you're back at work, notice how much more focus you can bring to your tasks.

CHAPTER 14

Facing Failure

I believe in all the ideas I've shared in this book. I practice all the tools I've detailed. But that doesn't mean I'm perfect—far from it. There are days that I fail to follow my schedule. Sometimes, I go out with friends, and I do not start the next day with a clear head or get a good night's sleep. When one of the kids is sick, I might have to skip a workout. You don't want to know how many times I've intended to sit down to write one of these chapters only for something to come up.

Every single year, when I review my tasks and my goals, I find there are areas I fell short. There are things I wanted to accomplish that just didn't come together for me.

I'm not alone in failing, of course. Every successful person fails sometimes. Take my colleague, Alan Smith. He's a Leeds United legend who started off in their academy. He was so good at such a young age that at fourteen he was chosen as one of the eighteen best players in England. Because of his promise, he was offered a place in a residential academy for the English national team. Imagine being told at fourteen that you are one of the best players in the country and your national team wants to mold you into a superstar.

He trained every day, stayed in dorms, went to a private school—nothing but the best for England's best and brightest. What an opportunity. But four weeks into his time at the academy, he quit. He failed. The truth is that, at fourteen, he missed home. He missed his parents, his brother, his town. He missed it all so much, he felt he had to walk away from that incredible opportunity.

So many people assume that failing once means failing forever. But Alan proves that's just not true. Three years after failing in the national team academy, he scored against Liverpool on his debut in front of forty thousand Leeds fans. He turned out to be one of only three players from the eighteen at the academy to make it as a pro.

Alan turned failure into a win—because he was absolutely determined not to let this failure define who he was. He doubled down and trained harder than ever. He went on to play in a Champions League semifinal, won the Premier League with Man U, came back from sustaining one of the worst injuries in the history of the Premier League, and had a twenty-year professional career.

He also made nineteen appearances for the national team.

Failure Is Good

One part of reviewing your progress that most people would rather avoid is inspecting where you fell short. Reviewing a highlight reel of all the times you crushed it is fun. Who doesn't want to spend an hour looking at all the big clients you signed or all the times you acted like parent of the year? But it's where you fail that often offers the most potential for growth and improvement.

Failure is not something you should fear or avoid. It's something you should seek out. Because failure suggests you're truly being ambitious and reaching for your highest potential. If you are not failing, then you haven't set yourself big enough goals. Failure is the benchmark for hard, barely achievable dreams. Without risking failure, you are condemning yourself to sit contently in your nice little comfort zone without ever taking a chance that could lead to true success.

If, during your reviews, you discover that you are checking off all your goals each day and each week with ease, it's time to go back and set the bar higher. If you have set New Year's resolutions and have completed them all by the next December—that's the real failure. It means that in some capacity you have wasted a year. You could have done more. A tougher goal could have led to a greater success, even if you ultimately failed to cross that ambitious finish line.

As a rule of thumb, you want to see a roughly 50 percent success rate for annual goals. Hovering around that point means you've tested yourself and you still have room to improve. At the same time, this doesn't mean you should make 50 percent of your goals impossible. It means picking goals that are extremely ambitious and barely achievable—the kind of goals that will require a real slog but that you know you can make progress on over the course of a year. For example, for the past six years, "finish my book" has been one of my annual goals. I failed for five out of those six years—but I kept making progress until I could finally check it off—which, if you are reading this now, means I actually did it!

Failing to be ambitious enough is a real risk in life. All you have to do is ask the teams that have gone from Premier League regulars to relegated also-rans. In 2020, Alan's Leeds United finally made it back into the Premier League. Not just that, but they made a real splash. Under the management of Marcelo Bielsa, they were playing some incredible soccer. But a season on, the results weren't going their way. The leadership at Leeds dismissed Bielsa for another ambitious manager, Jesse Marsch. When things failed to click right away, the whole club switched tack and went as safe as possible, appointing Sam Allardyce, a manager famous for scraping just enough points to stay in the league.

It wasn't enough. The team tumbled back into the Championship.

It would have been so much better to go down swinging and leave room to perform a miracle.

Reframing Failure

A couple summers ago, I was in New York interviewing former Manchester United assistant manager René Meulensteen. During our conversation, he told me about a particular moment he remembered very well. It took place in the locker room after United had failed to win the league.

Presiding over a room full of hung heads, Ferguson told the team to "never forget this feeling." Losing feels awful. If they didn't want to feel that way again, Ferguson told them, they needed to focus on winning next season.

They won the league the following year.

We often look at failure as an unconditional negative, but it doesn't have to be. We can reframe it to help us achieve our dreams. It does feel awful if you miss out on the promotion you were aiming for. It feels terrible when a relationship ends. Nobody wants to struggle with their mental or physical health.

In such moments, though, we should follow the advice of Sir Alex and focus on building new dreams out of our setbacks. Losing your job can open up the opportunity you were looking for to become an entrepreneur or find a career you actually care about. The end of one relationship may lead to the one you'll be in for the rest of your life. Or it may give you the time you need to focus on your health. If you are unhappy with your weight, this is the chance to find a workout and diet regimen that really work for you.

Failure is one of the world's greatest teachers. The best athletes, managers, entrepreneurs, and executives reframe failure to their advantage. They use it as inspiration and flip it around with a single word, "good."

"I lost my job—*good*. Now I have no option but to start that business I have been talking about for years."

"We lost our biggest account—*good*. They were a pain to deal with and demanded so much of our energy that our margins were terrible. We can focus our resources on higher-margin clients now."

"We lost the final—*good*. This will force me to train even harder in the offseason, so I never feel this way again."

This isn't just optimism for the sake of it. Refocusing on potential has the same value as visualization. Remember, our brains are programmed to look for what we prioritize—the same way we can pick out who said our name in a crowd—and that includes which mindsets we prioritize.

If you focus on seeing yourself as a failure or a loser, your brain will look for ways to confirm that feeling. This is one of the reasons depression can be so difficult to overcome. When you are depressed, your brain only finds reasons to be depressed. It won't let the light in.

Under most circumstances, though, we have the ability to tune our brains to a better frequency. A player who dwells on their failures when shooting with their left foot will never learn. A player who focuses on improving will become at least reasonably two-footed over time. Focus on the positive side of your setbacks, and you'll find the motivation and the opportunity to make sure your failure was only a temporary setback.

When Is It Right to Quit?

Of course, there are times when failure isn't meant to encourage us; it's meant to show we're heading in the wrong direction. Losing your job may not be a sign to double down and get a position higher up at a competitor; it may be a sign you need to work in a different field. A huge fight with your romantic partner may not suggest you need to double down and recommit; it may suggest it's time you both went your separate ways.

Those decisions are personal, and no one can tell you when it's time to make that huge decision. Soccer players famously struggle to accept the moment when they have to hang up their boots and find something else to do with the rest of their lives. However, one thing is certain. Whether you recommit to what you're doing or find something else to do, you should rely on the tools that have helped you achieve everything in your life so far.

We shouldn't aim to rise to the level of the competition; we should fall to the level of our training. In other words, don't rise to meet your goals, fall to the level of the systems you've implemented from this book.

No matter your goals in life, there will be setbacks. There will be times when you go down a goal in the opening minutes of the match. You'll lose some matches 4-0. It happens. Sometimes, it's a sign to change directions. Sometimes, it isn't. Regardless, your aim has to be to avoid dejection or panic. Instead, use the tools you already have in place to navigate your next step. Adjust your Big Three to accommodate your new reality. Continue to set aside ninety minutes to get through your crucial tasks. Practice the right skills, aim to improve, keep track of the score.

The plan is the same in the boardroom, in the office, and at home. Whether you switch careers or aim higher after a failure at work—whether you repair a relationship or look for love elsewhere—fall back to these systems and adjust them to meet the new moment. Plan your week based on your annual goals, write up your daily planner, turn off your phone, execute on your Big Three, rest, recover, and review for the following day. And repeat.

Remember, failure is not forever. On those days when I fall short—when I miss a workout or sleep in later than I intended—I know that I've only failed for that morning or day. Or that week, month, or year. Once that period of time is over, though, I can reset. I can get back to it. I can push through and keep going in whatever direction I feel is best. Because I know that the cycle is going to continue, and I'm going to get another shot, just like Alan did.

Game Time

Review the goals you've set for yourself in the short term and longer term. Rank them based on how ambitious each is. You don't need each one to be at the highest level of difficulty, but if none of them reach that level, consider how you can push yourself harder in certain areas.

You can also write down something that at the time you felt was a failure but turned into something great. Try and remember your feelings when experiencing that initial failure: Angry? Confused? Betrayed? Now fast-forward to the day when you realized this situation had turned into a success and those negative emotions had been a waste of time.

It's much harder but far more productive to reframe the failure using positive emotions. That way, whether the event transforms into success or not, you can reset, replan, and move forward.

CHAPTER 15

You Don't Have to Be Ronaldo

There have been many great players of the beautiful game—players that as kids we all want to be like. For me, it was Bryan Robson, Diego Maradona, and Chris Woods (look him up if you've never seen him play). When I first moved to America, girls marveled at Mia Hamm and Michelle Akers. For the next generation, it was Cristiano Ronaldo and Lionel Messi. These days, Kylian Mbappé and Jude Bellingham are delighting fans all over again. These are the players we love. They're the ones who end up on the back of the shirts we buy. They're the ones we pretend to be during a kick about with friends.

We never outgrow that desire to be a superstar natural talent who is the best there's ever been. Whatever field we're in, we want to be the best. That's great, but we have to recognize that in the years Ronaldo and Messi were facing each other in LaLiga, 218 other players were also suiting up to start each game in that league. A total of 500 or so were registered to play for those teams. All of them were making huge contributions to their teams, even if they weren't the best who ever played.

Put another way, 99.9 percent of professional players will never play at the level of someone like Ronaldo. There are about 2,760 professional players making up the 92 teams in the English soccer leagues. You might argue one or two of them are at that highest level or could get there someday, but everyone else will fall short.

And odds are the same is true of you. Whatever your career or life goals, it's unlikely I'm addressing this to the Ronaldo of your industry. If you happen to be a Ronaldo—or even the actual Ronaldo—first of all, congratulations, you probably don't need any more advice from me. And second, Ronnie, hit me up, and I'll send you a signed copy of the book. But assuming you aren't, the question is obvious: What's the point? What's the point of even trying if you can't ever be the GOAT?

The point is that you do not have to be Ronaldo; you just need to be the best version of *you*. The game you are playing is not a competition with the Ronaldo of your industry; it's *you* versus *you* every day. And unlike playing in the Premier League or LaLiga, that is a game that you can rig to guarantee victory.

All you have to do is follow your system: planning, performing, and reviewing/recovering as we've laid out in this book. Instead of judging yourself and your performance by how Jeff with the Porsche is doing, set the goals that are important to you. Plan to succeed in those areas, perform to your highest level, recover your progress, adjust your goals and process where necessary, and keep going. Did you make that extra call you promised yourself you would make before leaving the office? Did you keep up with the workout regimen you set for yourself for the year? Did you take that vacation you'd intended in order to recover some energy and remain focused for the rest of the year?

This doesn't have to just cover the ambitious plans you've set for yourself. You can judge your performance based off of the small things as well, such as whether you followed through on turning off your phone for an hour today.

Maybe someday this all leads to a world in which you have your own Porsche. Maybe not. But you'll have been a success on the highest possible level: the level you set for your life.

Your Best Can Make the Difference

You can't make yourself a Messi or Ronaldo. Players like that come around very seldomly, and while there's an immense amount of work that goes into reaching their incredible heights, undeniably, a large part of it is simply the luck of their unique genetics. They were born with a level of skill and fitness that you can never reach through effort and practice alone (although they undeniably also needed their incredible work ethics to reach those levels).

However, lacking their innate talent does not limit your ability to contribute to your success and the success of others. The thing is that these magicians are nothing without a team full of consistent seven-out-of-ten players putting in solid performances every week. That's right, those players who put in the work and show up every game with a quality performance are the only reason great players are able to be great. Messi can't win Ballon d'Ors, Champions Leagues, or World Cups without a team full of players who support him. Many of those seven-out-of-ten players accomplish incredible things through their hard work and graft. Those seven-out-of-ten players have long careers because teams need them. They are the engines, the cogs, the wheels, and the oil that keep the team moving.

As an aside, I know that earlier in the book I argued that you should force yourself to give an eight out of ten or a six out of ten for performance. That's really valuable when you need to make a call on whether you're putting enough in. But that doesn't mean you can't aim to give at least a seven out of ten each day. That will ensure you always get to round up to eight out of ten—because, truthfully, the value of your work will deserve it.

At times, teams need seven-out-of-ten players more than the superstars. When Ronaldo returned to Manchester United, everything had to revolve around him. It ended up destroying the team's morale and quality. The manager, Ole Gunnar Solskjaer, lost his job a little over one season into the experiment. Perhaps that team would have been far better off with a seven-out-of-ten striker in place of Ronaldo.

Whatever you're doing in life, you can always aim to be that seven-out-of-ten player every day. Consistency beats inconsistent moments of brilliance every time. Turning up on time, getting your work done, and seeing out your plan is what allows great things to happen. Those qualities may not get you the praise the superstars get for their final touch that wins the game, but without your performance, there is no game-winning goal.

Sure, Steve Jobs was a genius who changed the world, but he was only able to do what he did because he had a great team of workhorse engineers who made his vision come to life. Everyone wants to be a Jobs, but you can't become a Jobs; they just exist. What you can be is you, putting in seven-out-of-ten performances, creating the opportunities to raise that performance to eight out of ten and nine out of ten, which allows you to do your own remarkable things. Do you know who the CEO of Walmart is? Probably not, but they are running one of the largest corporations on the planet, even if they don't get the publicity of Jobs or Jeff Bezos.

Even if you don't love this advice, it's important to heed it as we round out your review of your performance—because acceptance of your potential and the work that is ahead is crucial to future planning and success. There are far more Steve Jobs wannabees in the graveyard of failed companies than there are workhorses. There are far more Messi wannabees with all the silly flicks and tricks you can imagine without a pro contract than there are seven-out-of-ten players with a contract at a club we'd all give anything to play for.

Those players are going to win trophies and live their dreams. Isn't that better than sitting at home and giving up just because you aren't Ronaldo?

Don't Take Shortcuts

Along with accepting our potential as seven-out-of-ten players, it's important to take a moment to address one of the ways the "wannabes" try to get around those limitations: they cheat.

Recently, a great player was suspended after testing positive for banned substances. After a few tough years in his career, including some injuries and struggling to get game time, it seems he was looking for a shortcut back to the best. The consequence is that he may never play again.

I doubt this player is alone in doing this. Many players are willing to do whatever it takes for a shot at greatness. But all the same, it's the wrong way to go about your career and your life.

There are few shortcuts to success. Everyone wants to lose weight quickly, get rich overnight, find the love of their life in an evening, and reach the top of their career in a blink. No one wants to do the hard work of a seven-out-of-ten player day in and day out.

But it doesn't work that way. The path I've laid out in this book—that's the way it's done. It's the way all successful players do it—the greats and the not-so-greats—and it's the way everyone in business and in life does it. Seven-out-of-ten daily performances give you a ten-out-of-ten life.

Be suspicious of anyone who tells you differently. It could come back to bite you.

There's No Final Whistle

If you follow all the advice in this book, you'll find there's likely a path to achieving all your goals. I hope you do achieve them—all of them.

But what do we do when we achieve those things? We often fail to think beyond the initial goals we set. We want to get the promotion or start our company. We want to run a marathon. But what do we do the day after those dreams come true?

The answer is the same one we had in the last chapter on failure: we return to the same system. There's always another game, always another season. There's always a new challenge ahead. Whenever you find success, do as the players do: celebrate, enjoy yourself, and then show back up to training, ready for the next challenge.

That's how we build on success and keep rising to our full potential: whether that's on the pitch, in the office, or at home.

Game Time

As you review your progress, make a conscious effort to continue to only compare yourself to your own performance from day to day, week to week, and so on. You're in a race only against yourself. If you use the scoreboard provided at www.soccerofsuccess.com, you will be able to track each month's performance against your best month to date, an easy way to play you against you without worrying about the other team.

PART IV

Extra Time: Leading a Team to Success

CHAPTER 16

The Need for Teams

The greatest sporting achievement of all time occurred just a few years ago.

One of the many reasons this is such an incredible story is that it had little to do with an individual. There are many fabulous sporting stories of individual brilliance in which a player or athlete overcame huge adversity to knuckle down, fight hard, and beat the odds. Muhammad Ali's comeback, Usain Bolt setting the record as the fastest man of all time, Jesse Owens winning the gold in front of Adolf Hitler. I'm sure you can name a few off the top of your head as well.

All of those stories can inspire us, but they're about one person doing something incredible. And they're about athletes at the top performing at the top. To get an entire team of underdogs to perform together far beyond their limit—and not just for one match but across an entire season—is almost unimaginable. Sure, teams can go on an unexpected cup run or upset a heavyweight favorite every once in a while, but to play at that level for thirty-eight games when no one thought they could do it? It's unheard of.

I'm talking, of course, about what Leicester City did in the 2015–2016 season. At the start of that season, Leicester was given odds of 5,000-1 to win the Premier League. That wasn't the bookies being dismissive. The Premier League is unforgiving. There are no easy games. It is ruthless at the top, and the only teams that have won the title in the twenty-first century have all been part of what we usually call the "Big Six." Since 2000, only five other teams have won the league: Manchester United, Arsenal, Manchester City, Chelsea, and Liverpool. Those also happen to be the biggest and best-funded teams in the league and some of the biggest clubs in the world.

So why would anyone back little old Leicester City? The season before they'd barely survived relegation. The season before that, they were in the Championship. This was a team that still fielded a squad mostly built in the Championship. There were no major all-stars. The consensus was that the very best the team could hope for was an easier path to staying up for another year.

The fact that the team won their first two games and were technically top of the league didn't really surprise anyone. They beat Sunderland who were destined to struggle that year, and West Ham, who would go on to have a good season but started the year poorly. A draw against Tottenham was a good performance, but by their seventh game of the season—when they experienced their first loss in their first game against a "big" side in Arsenal—conventional wisdom suggested this was the start of their drop toward the bottom half of the table where they belonged.

In most seasons, the conventional wisdom would have been right. But Leicester didn't listen to convention. The team followed up that loss with a ten-match unbeaten run, only drawing twice. At that point, nearly halfway through the season, the team was in first place. A loss to Liverpool took them to second, but after an away win at Tottenham two games later, the Foxes reclaimed the top spot and wouldn't lose it again for the rest of the season.

What Leicester achieved was unprecedented, and it was only possible because the team performed at a level greater than the sum of all its parts. There was no Ronaldo or Messi on that team. While Riyad Mahrez would go on to play for Manchester City, he wasn't on anyone's radar up to that point. Without a single superstar, the team had beaten some of the best opposition in the world. That's the kind of success a great team can offer you.

We Accomplish More Together

Before concluding this book, it's important to take a little time to expand the systems and values I've laid out so far and take them beyond you, the individual reader, to the teams you may be leading in an effort to accomplish your goals.

The reason you need to share these ideas with those who support your dreams is because everybody needs a team. We are tribal creatures, evolved to work together in order to survive. We naturally desire one another's company, seek out one another's feedback, and require one another's efforts to achieve our larger goals. Back in the days of our ancestors, being part of a team was the difference between living and dying. We had to hunt together; we had to defend together. Everyone had a role. Everyone had a purpose. Being part of a great team could mean the difference between merely surviving and thriving and progressing.

In the present day, life is more complicated. We have technology that allows us to work alone and do a great deal without anyone else's contribution. But we still need teams to take on anything particularly ambitious. It took a team to get a man to the moon. It took a team to build the internet. It'll take teams to solve climate change and build the next generation of technology. People like to trot out the expression, "It takes a village to raise a child," but it's so popular because it's true. We need the help of family and friends, teachers and neighbors, understanding employers and helpful government resources to successfully raise our children. It isn't a solo project.

Even if we are self-employed and enjoy working alone, we need a team. Take being an author. You may think it's a lonely, one-person job to crank out the pages of this book, word by word, thought after thought. But an author needs a team: you need a publicist, an editor, an agent, a marketer, and of course, a very patient and caring spouse who supports you and your crazy dream of writing a book (thanks, Tara). The myth of a solitary genius locked away from society to create their brilliant story is just that, a myth. Those writers were still meeting up with colleagues to discuss ideas, fine-tuning dialogue or descriptions with friends, and getting notes from family on how a chapter reads. It takes a village to write a book, the same way it does to raise a child.

Needless to say, the same holds true in soccer. This is a team game. No player, no matter how talented, could win in a 1v11 match. Lionel Messi playing against the Inter Miami U13 academy team would lose heavily. In fact, as we've already covered, even the great players require a team performing above the average to display their greatness and win matches.

So why do we try to do so much by ourselves in our everyday lives rather than embrace the power of a team? Most of us have around 40 working hours in the week. If we are extremely diligent in that week, we can make those 40 focused hours of work. However, if we used half of those hours to build, train, and mentor a team of 10, we could turn our 40 weekly hours into 240 hours. If we work alone for

40 weeks, we'll have 1,600 productivity hours. That team would have 9,600 hours of productivity. There's really no comparison, is there?

Becoming a Leader

Of course, to see the benefits of a great team, you have to lead that team to greatness. Leaders set the tone and help everyone on the team understand their role. There have been some fabulous leaders in soccer, managers and players alike. Think of the great managers like Sir Alex Ferguson, Pep Guardiola, and Leicester's Claudio Ranieri. Think of the great team captains like Roy Keane, Tony Adams, Patrick Vieira, Paolo Maldini, and Carles Puyol.

The managers and captains I just mentioned played for or managed different clubs, in different positions, in different countries. They all have different nationalities, as well as different leadership styles and traits. So what made them all great leaders?

That's a key question because if you want to take what you've learned in the hat trick of success and expand it into the Soccer of Success for a whole team, you need to be a great leader just like Keane or Puyol.

One thing that all these leaders have in common is that they recognize that in order to get the desired result from a teammate, you have to know what that person needs in order to reach their potential. One person needs a good "bollocking," while another needs an arm around the shoulder and a quiet chat. Some players respond to public criticism, while others shrink from it. And sometimes, what a player needs changes from moment to moment.

That's why leadership is tough. It is not a set-and-forget automated system. It deals with ever-changing emotions across a wide range of unique people.

To become an effective leader, you need to recognize the difference and distinguish the needs of one person from another. There is a business phrase: "Praise in public and criticize in private." It's good general advice, but it isn't always true. Instead, you have to use empathy and build the muscles to really read people and the moment.

You also have to build up the tools to communicate successfully with different people in different moments. For instance, there's a lot of value in the "sandwich" technique, in which you "sandwich" bad news or criticism between two pieces of good news or compliments. You might start by complimenting a teammate on their great presentation before mentioning the fact it came in a day late and you expect it on time next time. Then you can finish by reminding them that their work was exactly what you were looking for. That's usually a far more successful way to deliver news than to be bluntly critical. But again, not always. Sometimes, you have to be blunt—particularly with expectations.

No matter what forms of communication you use or how you tweak your leadership style, there is one hard and fast rule you can always cling to: great leaders lead by example. A great captain doesn't just tell the other players to play hard; they play harder than everyone else. If someone needed to jump into a tough tackle, Keane, Puyol, or Vieira were always willing to show how it was done first. They would never ask another player to do something that they were not willing to do themselves.

The same is true of being a good parent. You have to live up to the same kinds of behavior you demand of your children. You won't be very effective telling them to talk in a respectful tone of voice if you always go around yelling. They won't listen to your rules about doing homework on time if they see you struggling to get your work done on time. Employees are the same way. If you want everyone at work on time, you should arrive early. If you want everyone focused on work, don't let your team catch you on social media in the midst of a tight deadline.

In other words, model the behavior you want to see. For this same reason, there's real value in leading with calmness and enthusiasm. Both are contagious. As a leader, if disaster strikes (and it will), if you stay calm, the team will remain calm. If your child falls off their bike and scrapes their knee, if you respond calmly, they will calm down pretty quickly. When I used to coach young kids, one of them would inevitably get smashed in the face with the ball at least once a match. Just before the tears came, I would enthusiastically rush up to them and tell them "what a great header" that was. Instead of tears, they'd smile with pride and get back to the game.

To model calmness, take a step back from the situation and try to assess it soberly with some emotional distance. This leads those you're leading to naturally do the same. This is part of the value of managers in soccer: they aren't playing, so their physically induced adrenaline isn't running as high. They can make the right decision on a substitution, and their calm in the latter stages of a match can calm the players on the pitch.

The same value is found in modeling enthusiasm. You can be the person who always sees the positive side, never says die, and sees the good in every person, project, and task. That attitude can become part of the culture of your club, business, or home. Your enthusiasm can seep into the core of how others view the world. But only if you lead the way.

I know some of this advice might feel uncomfortable, but as a leader you have to be prepared to be uncomfortable at times. One of the worst things you have to do as a leader is let someone go, but when it's time to do that, make sure it's you that does it—no matter how uncomfortable it is. When one of your customers is upset and getting angry at someone on your team, don't leave them to handle it alone—take it on the chin and step forward to talk to the customer yourself. This shows your team that you have their back, making them more willing to work harder and hear you out if you have new ideas about how they should work.

That's the best way to introduce them to the ideas we've covered in this book. If you lead well, your team will want to incorporate the ideas that you've built into your life and your business. They'll want to work with what works for you.

And that's the first step toward building your best team.

Game Time

Look for opportunities to lead in your life and your work. Where can you step in and model the right behavior? Where can you show someone the value of the ideas we've covered already in this book?

Tomorrow, pick someone at work that you lead and give them the "ARM" technique: appreciation, recognition, and motivation. Something as simple as, "Hey, Sarah, I just wanted to let you know how much I appreciated you handling that difficult customer yesterday. The easy thing would have been to ask for my help. You handled it perfectly. Great job, and I'd like you to present your techniques at the next staff training seminar."

Remember, this can feel uncomfortable at first, but with practice, leadership becomes more natural.

CHAPTER 17

Building Your Best Team

The 2022 World Cup final has been cast as the culmination of Lionel Messi's whole career. Despite putting up perhaps the best individual numbers for any player in the history of the sport and accumulating an awe-inspiring number of winner's medals, there remained one thing keeping him out of the conversation for the greatest of all time: he'd never done it at the national team level. Argentina had come close to winning major tournaments during his time, but they'd never gotten it over the line.

Understandably, then, all the attention was focused on Lionel Messi for his part in the win over France. After all, he was the team's captain, and he did score two goals and hit the mark in the shootout after extra time. His contribution was not in doubt. But Messi didn't win that final on his own. It was his teammate, Ángel Di María, who earned the penalty that Messi scored in the twenty-third minute. Di María also scored the second of Argentina's three goals. Paulo Dybala, meanwhile, made a crucial contribution when he cleared a shot off the line in the late stages of extra time to keep the score tied. He also scored one of the penalties in the shootout. And the Argentine goalkeeper, Emiliano Martínez, put in one of the all-time performances between the posts. He made multiple saves during the game that kept France from winning the match outright, with one save coming in the final minute of extra time, allowing the game to go to penalties. Then, he saved one penalty in the shootout and psyched out another French player who sent his shot wide.

In other words, arguably Messi's greatest career achievement was only possible because he had the right team surrounding him. Without those particular players putting in particularly great performances, it's likely Messi never would have won that World Cup final.

Pick the Right Team

Your success is not just about having *a* team; it's about building the *best* team. And that requires you to build the team you need, full of players right for each role and hungry to succeed.

In business, life, and soccer, each position requires a different skill set for success. No team in the world would have any success with eleven strikers, eleven defenders, or eleven keepers—even if they were the top eleven players in each of those positions. You are not going to put Messi in goal no matter how good an all-around soccer player he is. Messi was never going to stop those shots that kept Argentina in the match. He needed his keeper to perform at *his* highest standard.

Not only that, but he also needed players around him who wanted to be part of that team and contribute to its overall success. We have all seen soccer teams filled with amazing individual talent that fail to win anything. Time and time again, big players go for big money without enough thought about whether they are the right player for that club. The Galácticos of Real Madrid struggled for years in the early 2000s to be even equal to the sum of their parts. Manchester

United has spent more on big-name players (including Ronaldo) over the last decade than almost any other team in the world and has barely managed to win a couple FA Cups, a Europa Cup, and two League Cups in that time.

On the other hand, clubs hovering around the bottom three often enter the transfer window knowing exactly what they need to "strengthen the squad." These clubs go out not to buy the biggest and best names but with a clear target for the type of player who could most contribute to the team. If they're short on goals, they might go out and recruit a big goal scorer to crawl their way out of the relegation zone. Veteran players are brought in who have a history of dealing with the relegation scrap. They can fight and inspire the younger players through the battle. The whole team is heavily incentivized behind one goal: "Stay in the league."

This strategy doesn't always work, but it provides teams with the best shot they have to stay in the league.

The same thing happens in other areas of the table. Well-run teams who think they have a good chance of actually winning the league go out and strengthen in their weakest areas. They're disciplined enough to turn down an all-star if that player would upset the locker room or change how the team plays. Smart recruitment can make the difference between finishing first and second.

All of which is to say, when building your own team, you need to find the correct balance that is required to achieve the goal in mind—whether that is a long-term or a short-term fix, and whether it's in life, business, or sport. Are you entering a heavy sales phase? Are you struggling to deal with your sales volume and need to iron out your operations and processes? Have you grown too big for your in-house bookkeeper and need to outsource to a firm or bring in a seasoned CPA? Have you reached a point that you need a new CEO with a set of skills to scale your company at a new level?

There is a great phrase on this topic that I love: "Hire slow, fire quickly." Typically, in business, we do the opposite and hire on impulse, only to keep people around that should have been let go long ago. I'm not pointing fingers here; I've been guilty of this as much as anybody. If we really want to build a great team, though, we need to think methodically about what our goals are, what our current team looks like, where we are weak, and what kind of personality fills that weakness—because personality is as important as the skills the new hire has.

A Team Is Only as Good as Its Worst Attitude

The greatest teams are the ones who push and challenge each other. They don't settle for average performances from anyone. They want to drag everyone up from a seven-out-of-ten performance to an eight out of ten. When a team member shows either an inability or unwillingness to perform at the set standard, the whole team recognizes that they have to be cut.

To create a team environment like that, you have to focus on an area many leaders ignore: values. So often, soccer managers and business managers focus entirely on the skills they need in their team. You need a left-footed center back and a right-footed center back. You need speed in your wingers, accuracy in your strikers, and a high soccer IQ in your midfield playmaker. But the reason many teams fail even with these skills in place is that the players lack the values required for winning. Values such as integrity, work ethic, courage, and grit rarely can be taught or changed. Sir Alex Ferguson famously used to go and visit the grandparents of youth players to see if those players truly valued hard work. They are part of someone's DNA or ingrained into them at an early age as much as their innate talent for the game. Similarly, abilities such as being a fast learner, being organized, and creativity are rarely teachable.

When your starting right back is out injured, the key to continuing your winning streak is having a player adaptable and ambitious enough to step into that role. They need to believe in hard work so they can put in the extra effort in a new position. They need creativity and courage to excel with unfamiliar responsibilities. They may lack some of the skills of the starter, but with the right values and abilities, they can cover until your starter is back. And sometimes, they can grow into the role so successfully, they become your new starter.

Having the right values also increases the ability to use the skills players were born with. Within each role, there's always room to build and continue to upgrade the skills that allow each team member to contribute.

Daily training, video analysis of your weaknesses, listening to your manager, coach, and fitness experts: as a professional everything is laid out for you. All you have to do is follow the plan. Easy, right?

Obviously not. We can all name players who had immense skill but failed to live up to their potential. Without the drive to succeed and a belief in being part of a team, even the most talented players will struggle for success.

That's why any team you build has to possess the right values and abilities as much as the right skills. Many skills—particularly outside of professional sports—can be trained. So long as you have the right kind of people in place who are adaptable and eager to win, it should be possible to develop the systems to train people to be their best.

How to Improve Your Team

With the right attitude and right people in place, you can improve performance by focusing on four things:

- Creating a common goal
- Taking action on the important stuff
- Implementing a scoreboard
- Practicing accountability

CREATE A COMMON GOAL

In the game of soccer, the most common goal is to win the game. But that isn't always the case. If you are playing Real Madrid away, the common goal for the team might be to "not lose," or even to keep the goal differential low. Over the course of a season, the common goal of one team might be to stay in the Premier League; another aims to win the FA Cup; a third is focusing on building up their young talent to improve the club's position and sell some players in the summer.

The important element of all these goals is that they are *common*, meaning everyone on the team agrees with them. The goal may come from the owner or the manager, but there is buy-in from everyone. When things get hard and tough questions are asked, the common goal can steady everyone, reminding them why they're doing what they're doing.

You can't overestimate how important this same quality is in life. Many families struggle when they aren't all on the same page. If one spouse wants the family's common goal to be increasing income or building a new business and the other wants to focus on raising children, this can create friction. If half the family really values sitting down to dinner together and the other half always wants to take the meal and sit in front of the TV, that's going to cause problems.

Businesses also struggle if the organization has no clear common goal. Are you trying to beat your top competitor? Are you seeking to offer the lowest price for your service? Do you want to have the best reviews? Is the aim to release a new product that changes the market? If everyone in the company is pursuing different goals, it's hard to keep everyone on the same page and driving toward the right result.

In other words, in soccer, business, and life, you want to have a goal that everyone shares. What deserves your laser focus while still keeping the other everyday items alive and active? What are you aiming to achieve within the next year? Answer that and make sure everyone on the team is signed up for the same goal.

TAKE ACTION ON THE IMPORTANT STUFF

In life and business, there is always "stuff" that has to be done to achieve the common goal. For a soccer team, that stuff might include working out, watching video, resting, and training. But some actions have more impact than others. To improve your team's performance, you should identify and act on the executables that have the highest impact of achieving the common goals identified. If this sounds a bit like your Big Three, you're right. We're expanding this to include the most valuable tasks for your team.

Every executable needs to check two boxes: it needs to be relevant (when carried out, it helps the team achieve their common goal), and it needs to be achievable (team members can execute them).

Consider the example of that team playing Real Madrid away. Their common goal is they don't want to lose. What task would help them best do that? Many managers would argue the team should get all eleven players to "park the bus" and play in the back third while defending for their lives.

Does this help the team achieve their goal? *Yes!*

Can all the players do this? *Yes!*

This is why it's such a common tactic. Parking the bus is not pretty, but it's effective when trying to avoid a loss and something every professional player can do.

Now let's say your company's common goal is to release a new product next year. You can't drop everything to push for this product because you'd lose revenue from selling and servicing existing products you've released. Instead, you might look to improve efficiency in your business-as-usual practices to free up forty-five minutes every day for the team to focus on that new product exclusively.

Would that help the team achieve their goal? *Yes!*

Can they do it? *Yes!*

For family, this might be as simple as setting aside TV time until after dinner and keeping phones off the table for dinner. Everyone could do that, and it would help the family achieve their goal of more time together.

In the real world, there's often some extra complexity to these situations, of course, but by trying to simplify things this way, you can find where a change can make the most impact on what everyone wants.

IMPLEMENT A SCOREBOARD

We've already discussed creating a scoreboard for your own goals. Here, you want the same thing for the team. In soccer, this is easy. Players, coaches, fans, and owners have the league table that constantly reminds them of their progress (or failure). But smart clubs also keep internal scoreboards for the players and staff to see that relate to their common goal. They will have a scoreboard for things like points from away games, away game draws, minutes in the first team for academy players, and so on.

For business, you might have a scoreboard that tracks sales. It might include the number of calls made or leads generated or new customers acquired or upsells attempted. The team should decide what will be on the scoreboard, but it has to be simple enough that everyone can understand the information at a glance. Essentially, you want the team to know in an instant if they're winning or if they're falling behind.

For your family, maybe you need a chart that tracks the number of dinners around the table each week. This can become a game in and of itself. Nobody wants to break a ten-dinner run. A scoreboard like that can also create space for incentives. Perhaps a successful month without any missed dinners at the table could end in a pizza night.

No matter what goes on the scoreboard, these metrics help everyone track how the team is doing and give visual encouragement to do a little better and a little more on the way toward that common goal.

PRACTICE ACCOUNTABILITY

To continue to improve team performance and cohesion, we need to add one final element. We need to have regular accountability sessions that keep the team on track with the common goal. Distraction is inevitable in life, even with the best teams. There will always be forces that try to knock us off course. Accountability sessions can allow us to reset and refocus on what really matters.

Traditional accountability sessions in soccer come in the form of video review. In today's world, video of a game is available almost instantly. Clips can be analyzed and played to the whole team in a matter of hours. Some managers have even been known to have the highlights of the first half ready to review at halftime to prepare the players for the second half. These sessions can allow players to see where they are falling short of achieving the common goal. A centerback can see how the opposition's striker keeps pulling them out of position and what they can do to prevent that from happening in the second half.

Accountability sessions in business are a little different. To start with, we don't usually have video. Instead, we can rely on our scoreboards, reviewing how we are tracking with our common goal. Are we seeing more sales calls? Are we upselling better? Are we completing those forty-five-minute sessions focused on our new product? Are those meetings showing progress on the product as we expected?

Where the team or an individual is falling short, these sessions allow us to dig into why. Perhaps an employee missed their sales call number because they were putting out a fire with an important client. That can lead to a productive discussion about how to minimize the issue that upset the client and systems that could allow the employee to get back to calls more quickly. It can also allow that employee to draw a line under the week and recommit to the goal for the next week.

A regular family meeting can also be a great chance to review progress on our common goal and catch up on what's happening in one another's lives—as well as how every member can help the others to move the family closer to where they want to get together.

Leaders Create New Leaders

There's one final way to improve your team: create leaders who can carry your goals forward without you. As we covered in the last chapter, building a team requires you to become a leader who lives up to the lessons of this book, shares the wisdom with your team, and helps them develop these systems themselves. But you can take this a step further by raising the right members of your team up to lead on their own.

Eric Cantona exemplified this philosophy. He was known to stay after practice, grab some bags of balls, and keep practicing. When the younger players in the class of '92—David Beckham, Ryan Giggs, and Paul Scholes, among others—started playing more first-team games, Cantona was a mentor to them. He helped them develop into the leaders on the pitch they would become.

This is one of the primary jobs of a leader. Managers often keep an eye out for a potential future captain. Many managers also notice those veteran players who might make great coaches in the future. In other words, they're constantly seeking out potential leaders and helping them develop the skills to lead. They put the spotlight on those players, trust them in the tough games, and give them responsibilities in the locker room.

In business, we can seek far and wide for those we want to mentor, develop, and help grow into leaders. We can hire them, promote them, train them, and give them additional responsibilities within the company. These new leaders can help us maintain discipline and focus. Like us, they can be an example to others and hold others accountable when we aren't around. They can represent the best of what the company's culture represents.

It's even possible to find leaders in family. Some kids are just natural leaders. There's often a sibling that leads the others, or a cousin who takes charge of the larger group. By entrusting them with more responsibility and a greater sense of purpose in taking care of the others, you can reduce the burden on yourself while providing the others with an example they can emulate.

With those leaders by your side—in life, in business, or in soccer—you can harness the potential within yourself and within your team to accomplish all you dream of.

Lead the way to using the entire Soccer of Success, and nothing can hold you back from winning.

Game Time

Review the teams in your life. Do you have the right personalities and values in place for success?

Ask the various members of your current teams in your life what they think the common goal of the team is and see if they all match or are drastically different.

As you mull this over, spend some time refining that common goal so you have one that everyone can buy into.

CONCLUSION

Three of my four kids play soccer. Not to brag, but they're pretty good. Sometimes, I get asked by other parents whether they'll go on to play in college or even go pro. I have to tell them that, honestly, I have no idea. Playing at that level requires a true love of and obsession with the sport. It will be each of their decision whether that's the right dream for them.

What I do know, though, is that even if each of them quits at age eighteen, they'll have developed some powerful fundamental skills and insights that will help them for the rest of their lives. Fundamentally, they'll know how to plan, perform, recover, and lead others.

My daughter, my one child who isn't interested in playing, has also absorbed many of those lessons. Simply by watching and growing up around the game, she's also learned many crucial principles that will help her achieve whatever she wants in life.

Aside from the entertainment, the joy, and the fun of the beautiful game, this is the lasting value of being a part of it. There's so much that soccer can teach us about living and succeeding. I hope I've captured some of it for you here.

For those of you who have never played soccer, I want you to know that it's never too late to take part and learn from the sport directly. I've seen leagues for over-forties, over-fifties, and over-sixties with many players who have barely ever kicked a ball.

And for those of you who aren't sure whether to really integrate the Soccer of Success into your life, I want you to know the same thing. It's never too late or too early to live these lessons. My seven-year-old son has taken it upon himself to write out his own daily schedule to keep track of how well he's using his time. Upon reading this book, my eighty-year-old mother told me she wished she'd had this advice earlier, but she was going to start using it now.

It's never too late to start getting more out of life. It's also never too soon to start moving toward success. With that in mind, please don't forget to check out all the additional resources available at www.soccerofsuccess.com. Those documents are designed to help you start using the Soccer of Success today and making progress toward your goals immediately. And as you make that progress, I'd love to hear from you. Feel free to send stories and questions to ciaran@soccerofsuccess.com.

The best thing about soccer is that there's always another game— win, lose, or draw, you always have the chance to do better next time. With a little more planning, a better performance, and some time to rest and review, the next game can really be the one you make count.

Good luck.